Government in Modern Ireland

GOVERNMENT IN
MODERN IRELAND

Muiris MacCarthaigh

IPA
INSTITUTE OF PUBLIC
ADMINISTRATION

First published in 2008
by the Institute of Public Administration
57–61 Lansdowne Road
Dublin 4
Ireland

www.ipa.ie

ISBN: 978-1-904541-72-1

British Library cataloguing-in-publication data
A catalogue record for this book is available from the British Library

Cover design by sin é design, Dublin
Typeset by Computertype, Dublin
Printed in England by Cromwell Press, Trowbridge, Wiltshire

Contents

Acknowledgments

The Irish state is constantly evolving. Monitoring and understanding changes within governing institutions and administrative processes present obvious challenges. I am therefore indebted to the following for their comments and suggestions: Sean Brolly, Ciaran Byrne, Andrew Campbell, Pamela Carson, Dermot Clynes, Kieran Coughlan, John Cullen, Anthony Cummins, Siobhan Egan, Claire Hamilton, Paul Haran, Niamh Hardiman, Katy Hayward, Tom Healy, Ann Higgins, Francis Jacobs, John Kennedy, Liam Kenny, Liam Kidd, Victor Laing, Frank Litton, Fergal Lynch, Maurice Manning, Barry McGinn, Patrick Millen, Jim Molloy, Art O'Leary, Dermot O'Sullivan, Robert Pye, Nicola Tickner, Barry Vaughan and Gavin Young.

Any errors or inaccuracies herein remain the responsibility of the author.

1

Introduction – Democratic
self-rule in Ireland

The Republic of Ireland is a parliamentary democracy of 4.3 million
people that has enjoyed self-rule since 1922.[1] How it is governed
remains a matter of constant debate and deliberation, and political
parties compete at elections for the right to control the principal levers
of state power. Rather than focusing on the political dimension of
government, this volume provides a necessary introduction to the
administrative framework within which governing takes place in
Ireland.

Often regarded as just a means of providing services sought by the
public, Irish public administration is in fact an indispensable part of the
structure of society; its composition and the *modus operandi* of all its
parts are a matter of concern to every citizen. Ensuring that the work of
the administration is aligned with the needs of the people is a key tenet
of democratic government, and as Chapter 2 details, a constitution is
normally used to provide a primary template for realising this.
Constitutions establish a framework for governing and, in particular,
provide for an executive to carry out the functions of government,
whatever they may be. Modern governments can be involved in a wide
range of functions (e.g. taxing, trading, regulation and resource
distribution) across many policy fields (e.g. health, defence, education
and agriculture).

---

[1] Under the terms of the Government of Ireland Act, 1920 Ireland was divided into two
separate jurisdictions – Southern Ireland (26 counties) and Northern Ireland (six
counties). In 1922 Southern Ireland left the United Kingdom to become the Irish Free
State. Article 2 of the 1937 Constitution claimed that the national territory consisted of
the whole island and nominated the state as Ireland or Éire (although in practice these
names were used to denote the territory hitherto encompassed by the Irish Free State).
The Republic of Ireland Act, 1948 changed the 'description of the State' to the
Republic of Ireland. The constitutional claim on the six counties of Northern Ireland
was, however, tempered by constitutional amendment in 1998.

While there is great variety in the method by which a state is governed and its administration is organised, most democratic states primarily employ a tripartite division of power between legislative, executive and judicial pillars. This division is principally associated with ideas that emerged in Europe during the eighteenth century, as models of government designed to curb concentration of power became popular. It was argued that if these three pillars acted as a check on each other, no single pillar or person could assume complete control. These ideas had a huge influence on the Constitution of the United States and the establishment there of presidential democracy, a system with more checks and balances than parliamentary systems. Today, almost all liberal democracies follow this basic formula, and the 1937 Constitution of Ireland enshrines it as the framework for the functioning of the Irish state.

Legislative power (the power to make law) is granted in the first instance to the Oireachtas, the components of which are elected directly and indirectly by the people. One house of the Oireachtas – Dáil Éireann – approves a government that is vested with executive power, i.e. the power to make decisions and carry them out, and this government must provide an account of its actions to that house. The lawfulness of these decisions can be tested in the courts by the judicial pillar. The judges who make up this pillar are appointed by the government and their independence is guaranteed under the Constitution. In certain circumstances, the judicial pillar can suspend legislation and strike down draft legislation approved by the legislature. However, the legislature may also in certain circumstances remove judges from office. As later chapters detail, while there are often tensions and stresses concerning the power and role of these institutions, this is nonetheless the primary system of checks and balances as envisaged under the Constitution.

Of course, citizens do not have the time or resources to ensure that all elements of their government and public administration are continuously running in an optimal fashion; therefore, in parliamentary democracies, representatives are elected to a parliament in order to act on behalf of citizens. Parliament is thus the key institution of Irish democracy, as it is within parliament that a government is formed and the assent of the people is bestowed on issues of public policy. The converse of this arrangement is that, if parliament fails to act according to the wishes of citizens, those elected to it can be removed and replaced at election time. While a territorially based system of popularly elected local government also exists, Ireland is a unitary state, i.e. power is centralised rather than being substantially shared between national and sub-national levels of governments, as occurs in a federal system. Figure 1.1 provides a basic depiction of the power relationships between the people, their local, national and European Union representative institutions, and the public service.

In order to ensure that the wishes of the people, as expressed through the institutions of state, are carried out, a vast system of public administration exists to implement, regulate, advise on and co-ordinate public policy. This system forms the main body of chapters in this volume as the contours of the modern state are explored. The substantial and fundamental policy areas of education and health are also examined separately here. These chapters illustrate that a simple distinction between private and public spheres cannot adequately describe the limits of the Irish state. In fact, the boundaries between public and private in Ireland have always been somewhat blurred, and at the outer and inner reaches of government are a wide variety of institutions, enterprises, charities and other private organisations endowed with public duties. Here also there are often tensions concerning democratic legitimacy, accountability and power.

Furthermore, identifying what functions are appropriate to domestic public institutions alone is a matter for regular consideration. The European Union (EU) has challenged traditional conceptions of national sovereignty, as its legislation now determines many aspects of citizens' lives and governments' actions. Also, students of Irish government have too often ignored the administration of Northern Ireland. The changing landscape of the island, particularly since the signing of the 1998 Good Friday (or Belfast) Agreement, determines that more than ever there is a need to understand a shared institutional heritage as well as commonalities and divergences in how governing takes place in the two jurisdictions.

Figure 1.1. *Formal framework of Irish government*

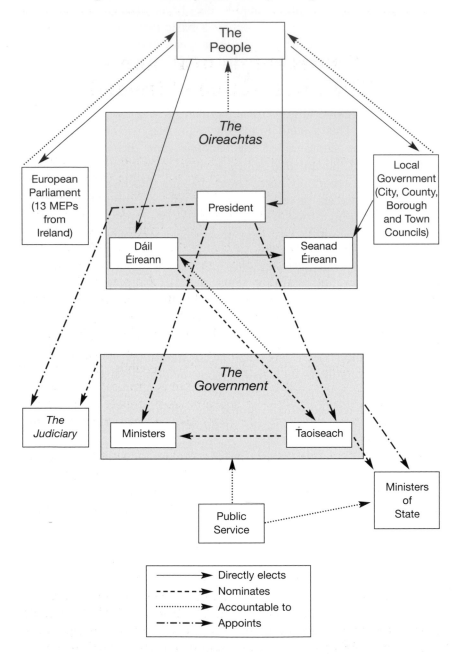

2

Bunreacht na hÉireann –
The Constitution of Ireland

Ireland is a liberal democracy. A simple interpretation of democracy is that it is a system of governing whereby the people (*demos*) are in power (*kratos*). However, though rooted in basic ideas of representation and accountability, democracy is a complex concept with many tensions between its various strands. Liberal democracy is concerned with maximising the individual freedoms of citizens in order that they can participate in decisions affecting power, while also offering protection for citizens against possible abuse of that power. The state is charged with pursuing collective goals for the common good, and a characteristic of liberal democracy is therefore an ongoing process of determining where the boundary rests between individual rights and the rule of law as enforced by the state. As well as being a liberal democracy, Ireland is also a republic. In a republic, the ideals of democracy are reinforced as the people, rather than an individual or institution (normally the king or queen in constitutional monarchies), are given sovereignty over the laws that govern them and the administration of the state.

Almost all democratic states have a written constitution (or basic law) to which all other law, e.g. property, criminal and family, is subservient. A constitution fulfils several functions. First and foremost, it establishes the rules as to how all the political institutions function and relate to each other. Secondly, it provides a framework for the law and the protection of individual rights. Thirdly, it establishes rights for those to whom it applies. Finally, in order for it to maintain relevance, a constitution should contain a method for amendment.

Ireland had three constitutions in the course of the twentieth century: the short Dáil Éireann Constitution of 1919, the Irish Free State (Saorstát Éireann) Constitution of 1922, and the current Constitution – *Bunreacht na hÉireann* or *the Constitution of Ireland*. The Constitution of Ireland was accepted by the people in a referendum (thus providing its popular legitimacy), and came into operation in December 1937.

5

Article 50 provided for all laws in existence prior to the new Constitution to come into force, provided that they did not conflict with the provisions of the Constitution. The sections of the Constitution are given in Table 2.1.[2]

Table 2.1. *The Constitution of Ireland*

Articles	Title	Subject matter
Preamble		
1–3	The Nation	Principal
4-11	The State	characteristics
12–14	The President	Institutions of state
15–27	The National Parliament	
15	Constitution and Powers	
16–17	Dáil Éireann	
18–19	Seanad Éireann	
20–27	Legislation	
28	The Government	
28A	Local Government	
29	International Relations	
30	The Attorney General	
31–32	The Council of State	
33	The Comptroller and Auditor General	
34–37	The Courts	
38–39	Trial of Offences	
40–44	Fundamental Rights	Citizens' rights
40	Personal Rights	
41	The Family	
42	Education	
43	Private Property	
44	Religion	
45	Directive Principles of Social Policy	
46	Amendment of the Constitution	Amendment
47	The Referendum	
48–50	Repeal of Constitution of Saorstát Éireann and Continuance of Laws	

---

[2] The full text of the Constitution is available online at www.oasis.gov.ie/government _in_ireland/the_constitution

Some of the principal characteristics of the state identified in Articles 1 to 11 are the name of the state, the national flag (green, white and orange), the official languages (Irish and English) and entitlement to citizenship. The institutions of state described in Articles 12 to 37 will be examined in later chapters. For now, it is important to recognise that as with constitutions in other states, Bunreacht na hÉireann does not mention some of the real sources of governing power. For example, there is no mention of political parties, which are the medium through which all political institutions of state – from local government to parliament – operate. Nor is a core institution of government – the Cabinet – mentioned. Similarly, in classic 'separation of powers' mode, the Constitution states that the government shall be 'responsible to Dáil Éireann' – a constitutional fiat that belies the reality that government largely controls Dáil Éireann.

The 1922 Constitution had been innovative insofar as it introduced ideas of fundamental rights and judicial review to a polity that was previously governed under the supreme authority of parliamentary sovereignty in London. The 1937 Constitution also establishes the fundamental rights of Irish citizens (in articles 40–44), which cannot be undermined by law or executive action. These include religious freedom, equality before the law, the right to own property and the right to education. Further rights have been discovered through the processes of judicial interpretation and referendums (see below). Article 45, concerning the 'Directive Principles of Social Policy', reflects the principles it was believed in 1937 that the state should adopt in its development of welfare policy in the socio-economic field, including justice and charity (Article 45.1). Constitutions are always forged in the context of evolving political and social conditions, and the 1937 Constitution has often been regarded as more confessional in tone than its predecessor.

Amendment and development of the Constitution

Despite the significant changes in Irish society over the past decade, the 1937 Constitution remains fundamental to our understanding of the governing process. In order that they retain popular acceptance and reflect social change, constitutions must contain a mechanism for amendment. In Bunreacht na hÉireann, the principal mechanism for changing the text is the referendum (Articles 46 & 47). For a referendum to be successful, a simple majority of votes cast is adequate. From 1937 to 2007 there were 28 proposed amendments to the Constitution, mainly concerned with EU affairs, moral issues, voting rights, citizenship matters and issues relating to Northern Ireland. The people have approved 21 of these proposals.

The text of the Constitution is not sufficient, however, to guide all actions of government and the public administration. Likewise, it is not possible to prescribe every right of each citizen in a single document. The Constitution therefore also provides for *judicial review*, i.e. the power of the courts to judge the constitutionality of legislation or the acts of a government official. In other words, if the High Court or Supreme Court (see Chapter 15) discovers that legislation or activities of the public service are in conflict with the Constitution, they can be deemed null and void. Unlike amendments to the actual text of the Constitution, judicial review is concerned with the meaning or interpretation of constitutional provisions.

There are two principal ways in which matters for judicial review come before the courts. Firstly, under Article 26 of the Constitution, the President can refer a Bill (or part of a Bill) to the Supreme Court to 'test' its constitutionality in advance of his or her signing it into law (see Chapter 3). Alternatively, a citizen can pursue judicial review of a particular law or government activity. In order to do so, he or she must have *locus standi*, i.e. they personally stand to be adversely affected by a law or state activity. However, *locus standi* has on occasion been extended to interest groups or to individuals who embark on judicial review proceedings on behalf of the general public. More than referendums, judicial review cases have played an enormous role in the development of the 1937 Constitution and its relevance to contemporary government and law-making. In particular, there have been considerable developments in respect of Articles 40–44 dealing with citizens' rights. By allowing the Supreme Court to discover hidden or 'unenumerated' rights, it has also underpinned the role of that court as interpreter and guardian of the Constitution.

In the Republic of Ireland, the ability to make the laws within which all activities of the state and its citizens must operate is granted by the Constitution (Article 15.2.1) exclusively to the *Oireachtas*. The Oireachtas consists of three elements – the Office of the President, Dáil Éireann and Seanad Éireann. The last two of these – Dáil and Seanad Éireann – combine to form the Irish parliament. We consider each element in turn in the following chapters, beginning with the Office of the President.

3

The Oireachtas I:
The Office of the President

The President of Ireland (Uachtarán na hÉireann) is the head of state and represents the state domestically and internationally. Apart from his or her constitutional duties, the President serves to develop Ireland's social and cultural capital both at home and abroad. The Presidential flag (or standard) consists of a golden harp on a blue background and is flown at Áras an Uachtaráin (the Presidential Residence) alongside the national flag. Elections to the office are held every seven years, unless an incumbent is removed, resigns or dies. On six occasions since 1937, only one candidate has been nominated for the position. Under the Constitution (Article 12), candidates must be over 35 years of age and nominated in one of three ways:

- by at least 20 members of Dáil and Seanad Éireann
- by at least four city and county councils
- by themselves if they have already completed one term in office (no President can hold office for more than two terms).

Despite the fact that the President has a popular democratic mandate, and additional functions can be conferred on the incumbent by law, the Constitution determines that the role is a relatively powerless one compared to that of directly elected heads of state elsewhere. The President mainly acts on the advice and authority of the government, rather than having executive functions as is the case in France and the USA. In this respect the Irish President is similar to monarchical heads of state in other European states, where holders of the office principally perform ceremonial duties and altruistic functions that do not challenge the executive prerogative.

The principal functions of the office are often regarded as ceremonial, as the President has no power to refuse to perform them or to nominate alternative candidates. The requirement to appoint persons to various positions stems from both the Constitution and statutory provisions, and includes:

- the appointment of the Taoiseach (Prime Minister) on the nomination of Dáil Éireann
- appointing or removing ministers on the advice of the Taoiseach
- granting a dissolution of Dáil Éireann on the advice of the Taoiseach
- providing seals of office for senior members of the judiciary and commissioned military, the Attorney General, Ombudsman, and Comptroller and Auditor General.

Along with the two chambers of parliament – Dáil Éireann and Seanad Éireann – the Office of the President forms part of the Oireachtas, and all legislative proposals from the parliament only truly become law when they have been signed by the President. The President is also Supreme Commander of the Defence Forces (for more on this see Chapter 17), and receives credentials from diplomatic and consular representatives.

The Office of the President is not completely without power, and the Constitution provides for a number of duties where the informed judgement of the office-holder is required. These include the right to address the Oireachtas or the nation on a matter of public importance; referring a disputed Bill to the people for a referendum; and submitting and appointing members to his or her Council of State (see below). There are two further functions where the President can exercise discretion and that can have potentially pronounced effects.

1. The President may refuse to sign a piece of legislation into law if he or she believes that it is in conflict with the Constitution. The President can ask the Supreme Court to 'test' its constitutionality. Before doing so, the President convenes the Council of State (see below). If the legislation appears before the Supreme Court, it can decide whether or not it contravenes the Constitution. This has happened on at least 15 occasions since the first President was appointed in 1938, though in most cases the legislation was deemed constitutional and was signed into law.
2. The President can refuse to dissolve Dáil Éireann if he or she believes that the Taoiseach requesting the dissolution does not have control of a majority of the 166 seats. This has never happened in practice, although the potential did arise in 1982 and again in 1992.

The *Council of State* can be convened by the President to offer advice. It has no powers. Articles 31 and 32 of the Constitution establish the make-up of the Council. It may consist of:

- the Taoiseach
- the Tanaiste
- the Chief Justice
- the President of the High Court
- the Chairs of both the Dáil and Seanad
- the Attorney General
- any former Presidents, Taoisigh or Chief Justices willing to participate
- up to seven Presidential nominees.

In case the President is abroad or unable to fulfil his or her functions, the Constitution provides for a three-person *Presidential Commission* to discharge the functions of the President, such as signing legislation. The three persons are:

- the Ceann Comhairle (chairperson) of Dáil Éireann
- the Cathaoirleach (Chair) of Seanad Éireann
- the Chief Justice.

The have been eight holders of the office since the election of the first President in 1938:

- Douglas Hyde (1938–45)
- Sean T. O'Kelly (1945–59)
- Éamon de Valera (1959–73)
- Erskine Childers (1973–74)
- Cearbhall O'Dalaigh (1974–76)
- Patrick Hillery (1976–90)
- Mary Robinson (1990–97)
- Mary McAleese (1997–present)

4

The Oireachtas II:
Dáil Éireann

The Irish parliament (often referred to as the Houses of the Oireachtas) sits in Leinster House in Dublin. It has two chambers – *Dáil Éireann* (the House of Representatives) and *Seanad Éireann* (the Senate or Second House). Dáil Éireann is the most important political institution in the state and fulfils several key functions. In no particular order, these include:

1. representing the electorate
2. the election and oversight of a government
3. processing legislation
4. deliberating and deciding on issues of public policy
5. allocating public money and scrutinising its use.

Representing the people

States cannot be run by referendums or direct democracy, and legislatures offer a means of aggregating the wishes of the population. As the members of Dáil Éireann are directly elected by the people at least once every five years, its work carries symbolic significance as it is based on the democratic will. The Constitution states that there shall be one member of the Dáil (Teachta Dála or TD) for every twenty to thirty thousand people (Article 16.2.2). A general election to a new Dáil must take place within 30 days of the dissolution of the old Dáil, and the new Dáil must convene within 30 days of the election.

Dáil Éireann is the principal body under the Constitution in relation to taxation, public expenditure and legislation. Its members have a duty to maintain the stability of the state and its institutions and ensure that public services function properly. In order to enhance its legitimacy, Dáil Éireann should reflect as closely as possible the make-up of the general population. However, it is undoubtedly true that the Dáil does not proportionally represent women, minority groups or the various socio economic levels within society.

The legitimacy of parliamentary politics requires a two-way process of communication. Not only do members of the Dáil represent and act on behalf of their constituents, but they are also charged with communicating to the population (sometimes via the media) the decisions of parliament and the purpose of new laws and regulations.

Election and oversight of government

The most important feature of parliamentary democracies is the fact that the parliament elects or approves the executive pillar of state. This is the essential difference between a parliamentary and a presidential system. In the latter, the executive (the President) is elected separately and is institutionally independent of the legislature.

The 166 members of Dáil Éireann are elected through the use of an unusual electoral system known as proportional representation by the single transferable vote (PR-STV). It is premised on the idea that the number of seats won by parties in the chamber should reflect as closely as possible the number of votes won nationally. Since 2005, the state has been divided into 43 constituencies for this purpose. When counting of votes in all constituencies is complete, the 166 members sign the Roll of Members in Dáil Éireann and take their seats. Most TDs will be members of a political party and will group together to form parliamentary sub-units for purposes of organisation, action and voting on issues.

The first vote in parliament following a general election is to select the *Ceann Comhairle* or Speaker of the House. The Ceann Comhairle is usually a senior member of Dáil Éireann and the main function of the office is to ensure that the Standing Orders (rules of procedure) are adhered to. Otherwise, the House would not be able to conduct its work efficiently. The interpretations of Standing Orders by the Ceann Comhairle are known as 'rulings'. The Ceann Comhairle presides over all sittings and may be substituted by the Leas-Ceann Comhairle as required. In the absence of the Leas-Ceann Comhairle, there is a panel of deputy chairpersons drawn from all parties. Ministers and ministers of state may not be on this panel. To ensure that the office is not politically partisan, the Ceann Comhairle is automatically elected to the Dáil at the next election, if he or she wishes to remain a member.

As detailed in Chapter 7, the Dáil then votes on who should assume the position of Prime Minister or Taoiseach. Once the new incumbent has received his or her seal of office from the President, he/she nominates members of the Dáil (and up to two members of the Seanad if necessary) to fill the 14 ministerial portfolios. Once the nominations are approved by the Dáil, they in turn are formally appointed by the President. Thus a new government is formed which is responsible to the Dáil for its actions.

The general arrangement for seating is: facing the Ceann Comhairle, the government benches are on the right; the main opposition party sits to the left; the smaller opposition parties and the independent (non-party) members sit on the backbenches immediately in front and to the left of the Ceann Comhairle.

Figure 4.1. *Seating arrangements in Dáil Éireann*

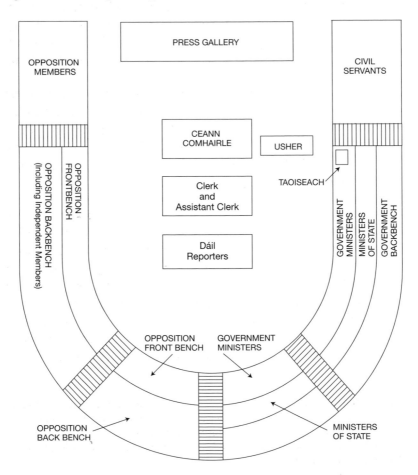

Procedures in the Dáil

There are five sources for the procedures of Dáil Éireann.

1. Article 15.10 of Bunreacht na hÉireann gives each House the right to 'make its own rules and standing orders'.
2. In certain areas, statute law (i.e. law passed by the Oireachtas) can have a bearing on procedure, but the constitutional protection given to each House to create its own rules has primacy.
3. The day-to-day procedure of parliament takes place within a set of rules titled 'Dáil Standing Orders relative to Public Business'. The standing orders are amended by the Dáil from time to time, on the recommendation of the Committee on Procedures and Privileges, or its Standing Sub-Committee on Dáil Reform.
4. Sessional orders, which are distinct from standing orders in that they terminate with the life of a parliamentary session (usually the length of a government's term in office), may be used. Sessional orders are often used to experiment with potential new standing orders.
5. The Ceann Comhairle has the authority to interpret Dáil standing orders and to rule on matters not covered in them. For this the Ceann Comhairle has a book of rulings based on precedent, which is updated as new circumstances arise. The Ceann Comhairle is not bound by precedent but seeks to be consistent with previous developments.

Under standing orders, the Taoiseach has the prerogative of deciding the items of government business to be taken each day, and their order. This usually follows a meeting between the parliamentary party 'whips' – members of each party responsible for the organisation and attendance of their respective party colleagues. They meet weekly in private to discuss how business is to proceed in the House the following week. The government Chief Whip[3] then draws up a document known as the 'Order of Business' for each day's sitting. The Order of Business lists the legislation to be debated, the motions to be discussed and any

[3] The Chief Whip is usually also a minister of state at the Department of the Taoiseach. His or her role is principally to manage government business in the Dáil, including the legislative programme, and to ensure that the members of the governing party or parties are present for all votes as necessary. The Chief Whip also has functions in relation to the Central Statistics Office.

other proposals to be put to the House (see Table 4.1). Each party whip will draw up a paper (confusingly also known as the 'whip') that will indicate whether or not a party member needs to be present for votes on different matters. A 'three-line' whip – i.e. a sentence with three lines underneath it – is the most important, and means that the TD must be present in the chamber for the debate.

The Journal Office in Leinster House also publishes daily a green-coloured Order Paper, which contains the Order of Business as well as details on all issues before the House that day. The General Office publishes a separate dove-grey Question Paper each day the Dáil sits, which gives the questions that are to be asked of the government. Deputies also automatically receive copies of new or amended Bills and a list of any amendments to Bills that are to be taken that day.

According to Dáil Standing Order (DSO) 21, the normal sitting hours of Dáil Éireann are as follows:

- Tuesday from 2.30 p.m. to 8.30 p.m.
- Wednesday from to 10.30 a.m. to 8.30 p.m.
- Thursday from to 10.30 a.m. to 4.45 p.m.

Of course these hours may vary depending on the workload and the decision of the government to extend the sitting times on any given day.

Once the Dáil elects the government, the government is constitutionally obliged to 'be responsible to Dáil Éireann' (Article 28.4.1). For the work of Dáil Éireann to proceed, there must be a quorum of 20 members present. There are various procedures whereby members of Dáil Éireann can hold government and individual ministers to account. We concern ourselves here with the most important of these – parliamentary questions.

Parliamentary questions
The principal method by which TDs (and typically those on the non-government party benches) attempt to hold government to account is via parliamentary questions (PQs). Two types of question may be put.

- *Oral questions* are asked orally in the chamber and, with the agreement of the Ceann Comhairle, may be followed by a supplementary question.
- *Written questions* are responded to in written format, with no provision for supplementary questions.

Table 4.1. *Sample of Dáil Order of Business*

ORDER OF BUSINESS
Tuesday 18 December 2007

The Order of Business today shall be as follows:

No. 2 – Appropriation Bill 2007 Order for Second Stage, Second and Remaining Stages

No. 3 – Health (Miscellaneous Provisions) Bill 2007 Order for Second Stage, Second and Remaining Stages

It is proposed, notwithstanding anything in Standing Orders, that:

(1) the Dáil shall sit later than 8.30 p.m. tonight and Business shall be interrupted not later than 10.30 p.m.;

(2) No. 2 shall be decided without debate; and the Second and Remaining Stages shall be decided by one Question which shall be put from the Chair, and which shall, in relation to amendments, include only those set down or accepted by the Tánaiste and Minister for Finance;

(3) the Second and Remaining Stages of No. 3 shall be taken today and the following arrangements shall apply:

(i) the proceedings on the Second Stage shall, if not previously concluded, be brought to a conclusion at 9 p.m. tonight;

(ii) the proceedings on the Committee and Remaining Stages shall, if not previously concluded, be brought to a conclusion at 10.30 p.m. tonight by one Question which shall be put from the Chair and which shall, in relation to amendments, include only those set down or accepted by the Minister for Health and Children;

(4) Private Members' Business which shall be No. 16 – Competition (Amendment) Bill 2007 – Second Stage, and the proceedings on the Second Stage thereon, shall also take place tomorrow on the conclusion of the Statements on the European Council, Brussels, and shall, if not previously concluded, be brought to a conclusion after 90 minutes on that day;

(5) Parliamentary Questions next for answer by the Taoiseach on EU matters shall be taken on the same day as the Statements on EU Council Meeting, Brussels, scheduled to be taken on Wednesday, 19th December, 2007, and shall be moved to be taken first as ordinary Oral Questions to the Taoiseach on that day;

Questions (2.30 p.m.)

Taoiseach: 1–51

Minister of State Kitt: 52–60

No. 2 – Appropriation Bill 2007 Order for Second Stage, Second and Remaining Stages (without debate)

No. 3 – Health (Miscellaneous Provisions) Bill 2007 Order for Second Stage, Second and Remaining Stages

No. 16 – Competition (Amendment) Bill 2007 - Second Stage (over 1 week)

There are sub-categories of oral questions:

- questions to the Taoiseach
- ordinary questions
- priority questions
- private notice questions
- leaders' questions.

Questions to the Taoiseach are the most commonly televised part of the parliamentary timetable as the leaders of the opposition parties question the Head of Government on a range of issues. Questions to the Taoiseach occur on Tuesday and Wednesday only, at 2.30 p.m. and 10.30 p.m. respectively.

Ordinary questions must be submitted at least four days in advance, in order for information to be gathered for reply. They occur from 3.15 to 4.15 p.m. on Tuesday and Wednesday, and from 2.30 to 3.50 p.m. on Thursday. There is a rotation process whereby the ministers appear in an agreed order to answer questions. Each minister can expect to answer questions for one day every five weeks. If an oral question is not reached, a written reply is submitted. No member can ask more than two questions, and the questions are chosen by lottery. The Ceann Comhairle decides whether or not a question asked of a minister is appropriate to the responsibilities of that minister, and questions cannot be repeated within four months.

Written questions form the bulk of questions put before the House and are also subject to the above rules, except that a question may be repeated after two weeks. They must be submitted three days in advance and the answer will be provided to the questioning TD, as well as being recorded in the official report of debates.

Priority questions are tabled by a member of a recognised parliamentary group of seven or more members. Only five can be asked in any sitting day; they are usually related to current affairs and are asked in the opening part of the sitting day rather than during ordinary question time. They must be submitted at least three days in advance.

Private notice questions (PNQs) must relate to a matter of 'urgent public importance' and must be submitted before 2.30 p.m. on the day they are to be answered. If the Ceann Comhairle permits it, the PNQ is usually asked at the end of ordinary questions.

Leaders' questions: Since 2001, the opposition party leaders are allowed to raise questions relevant to the business of the day. Time (21 minutes) is now allowed on Tuesdays and Wednesdays prior to public business for leaders of parties of seven or more members (two such parties exist in the 30th Dáil) to ask the Taoiseach questions.

The other mechanisms whereby the government is scrutinised occur through the performance of the other main roles, i.e. processing legislation and deliberating motions. We shall now consider these in turn.

Processing legislation

Producing legislation is a key function of parliament. In debating legislative proposals, members of parliament hold the government to account, as opportunity is provided for public analysis of important public policy issues. In anticipation of such debate, ministers (who normally sponsor pieces of legislation) must be able to defend their proposals and to ensure that there is sufficient public support for them.

Like most other parliaments, the Houses of the Oireachtas devote most of their time to legislative matters. The Bills Office is responsible for printing and circulating all new legislation and amendments to legislation. Legislation may be introduced in either the Dáil or the Seanad. Table 4.2 gives the quantity of legislation promulgated (made into law) in Ireland in recent years.

Table 4.2. *Quantity of legislation passed by Oireachtas*

Year	Number of pieces of legislation passing into law	Number of sittings (days)
2007*	39	76
2006	42	96
2005	34	92
2004	44	102
2003	46	97

* 2007 was an election year, which curtailed sittings of the Dáil.

Primary legislation occurs in the form of either *Public Bills*, which are Acts of Parliament applicable to the general body of citizens within the state, or *Private Bills*, which apply to individuals or individual institutions. Private Bills are rare and mainly deal with issues related to individuals or private institutions that seek powers outside of, or in conflict with, the general law. Public Bills may be subdivided into (a) Bills initiated by the government and (b) those initiated by a member of the opposition or government who represents a group of not fewer than seven members (see Dáil Standing Order 114), which are known as *Private Members' Bills* (PMBs). Government Bills are by far the most common form of legislation and are proposed by a minister (or minister of state if the minister is absent).

> All primary legislation begins its life in the form of a Bill. When a Bill has been approved by the Oireachtas (Dáil, Seanad and President), it becomes an Act.

With the exception of PMBs, for a proposed piece of legislation to come into being it must first be approved by the Cabinet, where the minister responsible for it argues the case for the necessity of the law. For example, every year the Finance Bill (which implements the measures in the Budget) is proposed to the Cabinet by the Minister for Finance. Once a proposal receives Cabinet approval, and has been drafted in the Office of the Parliamentary Counsel to the Government (see below), the Bills Office in Leinster House publishes a text and circulates it to all members. The government sets a date for initiating the debate on the Bill's contents in the Houses of the Oireachtas. There are five stages in the process of a Bill through the Dáil and Seanad.

Stage 1: The Ceann Comhairle must first approve the text of the Bill and its purpose (this is known as the long title). One of two procedures then occurs. The Bill may be published and presented to the Chamber by a Minister, Minister of state or member of a recognised group of members. Otherwise, any member is entitled to request permission to introduce a Bill to the House. If permission is granted, the Bill is published and circulated. No amendments are taken at this stage. An example of the former (and more common) form of Stage 1 procedure is given in Table 4.3.

Stage 2: This is where the general principles of the Bill are debated. There is no debate on the detail of the Bill at this stage, but amendments to delay the passing of Stage 2 may be proposed. The proposer may speak for 30 minutes, as may representatives of the other recognised groups. Other members may speak for 20 minutes and the proposer may reply for 15 minutes.

Stage 3: This is known as the *committee stage*, so called as it takes place among a small group of either Senators or TDs, depending on the House where the Bill is initiated. It is arguably the most important stage in the process, as it is in the committee stage that the amendments to the Bill are proposed and either accepted or rejected. The Bill is

Table 4.3. *Sample of Stage 1 procedure*

Local Government (Roads Functions) Bill 2007

Order for Second Stage.

Bill entitled an Act to provide for and to facilitate the transfer of certain functions from the Minister for the Environment, Heritage and Local Government to the Minister for Transport in respect of roads, to provide for the payment of moneys out of the local government fund to the Minister for Transport in respect of certain matters and to provide for related matters.

Minister for the Environment, Heritage and Local Government (Deputy John Gormley): I move: 'That Second Stage be taken now.'

Question put and agreed to.

Source: Dáil Debates, 13 November 2007.

examined section by section and schedule by schedule. Where amendments are not agreed, a vote may be taken among the members present. In order to save time and avoid repetition, the Chair may often 'group' the amendments that he or she considers to be related for the purposes of debate.

The Office of Parliamentary Counsel to the Government drafts government amendments. The minister may accept opposition amendments or agree to accept the spirit of these amendments and return at the next stage of the Bill (report stage) with amendments drafted by the Office of Parliamentary Counsel.

Stage 4: This is known as the *report stage*, where the Bill as amended (if at all) is presented back to the House. At this stage, there can be further amendments to sections of the Bill amended at committee stage or where the minister has indicated at committee stage that he or she will come back to an issue at report stage. No new section may be introduced at report stage unless it has been mentioned in committee. However, a new matter may be introduced that has not been mentioned, if the House agrees to it. In this instance the House formally recommits the Bill to committee stage to deal with the new amendments, and when these are dealt with the Bill reverts to the report stage.

Stage 5: After report stage is concluded the Bill is read for the final time (fifth stage). This stage is a formality; there are no amendments.

Once the fifth stage is passed, the Bill has been passed by the House concerned and if it is a Dáil Bill it is sent to the Seanad, or if it is a

Seanad Bill it is sent to the Dáil, where the process is repeated (other than the first stage). When the Bill is passed by both Houses it is sent to the President for signature if it was not amended by the second House it went to. Otherwise it goes back to the first House for consideration and subsequently to the President.

Under the Constitution (Articles 21.1 and 46.2), all Money Bills (i.e. Bills that deal with taxation and expenditure) and Bills to amend the Constitution must begin their life in the Dáil.

If the Bill is a Private Member's Bill (PMB), i.e. proposed by a member who is not a member of the government, it proceeds through the first two stages in the Dáil during Private Members' Time, i.e. the three hours a week allocated for TDs who are not members of the government (and are usually members of the opposition). A Private Member's Bill that involves a charge on public funds requires a special money message from the government. Most PMBs are defeated at second stage.

During the passage of legislation, the members of the opposition will debate and argue with the government member and attempt to extract as much information as possible about the actions of the government. The legislative process is therefore a key part of Irish public life not just for the purpose of law-making but also for holding the government to account.

When it comes to deciding on matters put to the Dáil by the Ceann Comhairle, all TDs have one vote each. When a question is put to the House by the Ceann Comhairle, responses are first given orally by those present. If the result is not clear or a deputy challenges the result, a *division* is called. A minimum of ten TDs are necessary to force a division or vote. Since 2002, divisions (voting) in Dáil Éireann can take place electronically as well as manually. Bells are rung in Leinster House calling TDs to vote and, after a few minutes, the doors to the chamber are locked and the vote taken. Normally, the bells ring for six minutes and after a further four minutes the door is locked. (This time is reduced to three minutes overall for a second electronic vote taking place immediately thereafter.) Tellers are appointed to count the votes and record the final result. If there are equal numbers of members for and against a motion, the Constitution gives the Ceann Comhairle a casting vote to decide the matter.

As well as primary legislation, the Houses may approve or annul secondary legislation, normally known as *statutory instruments*. A statutory instrument is a power to do something specified by enabling provisions in primary legislation; statutory instruments may be referred to as orders, regulations, by-laws, rules or notices. Statutory instruments are normally provided to persons (such as ministers) or institutions (such as local authorities) by primary legislation; when enacting or using them, the person or institution in question cannot go outside the provisions and intentions of the primary legislation.

Deliberation over motions and resolutions

As well as debating legislation, Dáil members debate motions on matters of concern and pass resolutions. Issues that arise and require discussion in the Dáil are dealt with as *ad hoc* motions. Individual members may propose motions for debate, which lead to expressions of opinion on matters, but they do not take precedence over government business. The time allowed for debate on a private member's motion, but not any stage of a Private Member's Bill, is restricted to three hours in the Dáil per week (Dáil Standing Order 115 (1)).

Under Dáil Standing Order 21(3), TDs may raise issues that relate to a particular minister's department through a 'Motion on the Adjournment of the House'. This takes place after the normal business of the House on Tuesdays, Wednesdays or Thursdays. Only four matters can be raised on any one day and the discussion lasts for ten minutes per issue – five minutes each for the TD who raises the matter and the minister who replies. No vote is taken, as the issue is purely for debate.

An example of an adjournment debate being selected is given in Table 4.4.

Under Dáil Standing Order 32, there is also provision for a debate on a matter of *'urgent public importance'* during a sitting day. It allows a TD to seek permission from the Ceann Comhairle to move a motion on the adjournment which is to do with 'a specific and important matter of public interest requiring urgent consideration'. The Ceann Comhairle receives notice of the member's wish and before the Order of Business for the day, the proposer reads out the reason for the need for the debate. The Ceann Comhairle then informs the TD whether or not the debate will take place.

An example of the use of Standing Order 32 is given in Table 4.5.

Voting public money and scrutinising its use

Running the state's affairs is an enormous task and requires vast amounts of money. This money is raised mainly through taxes.

Table 4.4. *Selection of an adjournment debate*

Adjournment Debate Matters.

An Leas-Cheann Comhairle: I wish to advise the House of the following matters in respect of which notice has been given under Standing Order 21 and the name of the Member in each case: (1) Deputy Michael D. Higgins – the urgent need to resolve the contradiction which has emerged between the Department of Education and Science and the Department of Justice, Equality and Law Reform regarding the rights of children whose parents are on student visas to avail of primary education in their locality; (2) Deputy James Bannon – the need for the Minister to provide urgent core funding for the continuation and expansion of osteoporosis services, which are currently provided by the Irish Osteoporosis Society, a charitable organisation surviving with a skeleton staff of two and which will be forced to close without such funding, leaving the public and health professionals without a point of contact; (3) Deputy Michael Creed – the issue of the forthcoming closure of a company in County Cork (details provided) with the loss of 120 jobs and to highlight the need for replacement industry; (4) Deputy Paul Connaughton – redundancies in the FÁS community employment schemes; (5) Deputy Joe Costello – the need to put an effective inspection regime in place to prevent extraordinary rendition flights passing through Irish territory; (6) Deputy Tom Sheahan – the need for the Minister to put funding in place (details supplied) to hold the invaluable services provided by a counselling service in County Kerry as a matter of urgency and to make a statement on the matter; (7) Deputy Martin Ferris – the failure to prevent illegal fishing by non-Irish vessels in Irish waters; and (8) Deputy Kieran O'Donnell – the need to promote the provision of IDA supported jobs in Limerick and the mid-west.

The matters raised by Deputies Paul Connaughton, Kieran O'Donnell, and Joe Costello have been selected for discussion.

Source: Dáil Debates, 12 December 2007.

Table 4.5. *Use of Standing Order 32*

Requests to move Adjournment of Dáil under Standing Order 32.
An Ceann Comhairle: Before coming to the Order of Business, I propose to deal with a number of notices under Standing Order 32. I will call on Deputies in the order in which they submitted their notices to my office.

Deputy Catherine Byrne: I seek the adjournment of the Dáil under Standing Order 32 to raise a matter of national importance, namely, the crisis

Table 4.5. *Use of Standing Order 32 (contd.)*

in the home help service. In the Rialto and Dolphin's Barn area alone, there are 37 people awaiting home help. Funding is not available from the HSE and it is unacceptable that a number of people will have to remain in hospital this Christmas because of the unavailability of the service. I ask the Minister to address their needs urgently.

Deputy Dan Neville: I request the adjournment of the Dáil under Standing Order 32 to discuss the following urgent matter, namely, the reduction in secure psychiatric beds at St. Brendan's Hospital by ten from 24, resulting in unacceptable circumstances in which there are no secure beds for very disturbed patients who cannot be accommodated safely in an open ward; and the fact that one disturbed person who recently appeared before the courts required a secure psychiatric bed but was released on bail when none was available.

Deputy Arthur Morgan: I seek the adjournment of the Dáil under Standing Order 32 to discuss the following matter of urgent national importance, namely, the ridiculous situation whereby the Minister for Education and Science is refusing to fund schools adequately while the Minister for the Environment, Heritage and Local Government is imposing massive water charges on already hard-pressed schools; and the need to achieve joined-up thinking at Government level and to clarify the situation whereby the Taoiseach is claiming the EU is imposing these excessive charges, while other members of the Government are stating the complete opposite.

Deputy James Bannon: I seek the adjournment of the Dáil under Standing Order 32 to discuss the following matter of national importance, namely, the threat to the education of primary school children in light of the financial burden placed on schools which are unable to meet the demand for excessive water charges levied on a piecemeal basis, without apparent logic or reason.

Deputy Martin Ferris: I seek the adjournment of the House under Standing Order 32 to discuss the following matter of urgent national importance, namely, the proposal by the EU Health Commissioner to impose restrictions on the importation of beef from Brazil on the basis of the report by the Food and Veterinary Office, and that this underlines the case for the Government to alter its position and call for a complete ban on Brazilian imports.

An Ceann Comhairle: Having considered the matters raised they are not in order under Standing Order 32.

Source: Dáil Debates, 18 December 2007.

Governments must seek the approval of parliament to raise taxes, borrow and spend money. The budgetary process is an essential part of government and is dealt with in some detail in Chapter 11.

For parliament, the presentation of the Budget by the Minister for Finance in December each year is an important part of the parliamentary calendar. It allows TDs the opportunity to discuss and debate how best to spend revenue raised by taxes. Like other policy matters, government proposals on financial matters are voted on in the Dáil.

A special committee – the Committee of Public Accounts (often referred to as the Public Accounts Committee or PAC) – is charged with ensuring that money voted by the Dáil for a particular matter was spent in the correct manner. To assist it in its work, the committee avails of the services of the *Office of the Comptroller and Auditor General* – an office provided for under the Constitution. The Comptroller and Auditor General's reports on public finance are presented to the Committee of Public Accounts, which itself makes an annual report (as well as some interim reports) to the Dáil on how public finances are being spent. The work of the Comptroller and Auditor General and the Committee of Public Accounts will be examined in more detail in Chapter 11.

Staff of the Houses of the Oireachtas

The work of Dáil Éireann and Seanad Éireann is assisted by a secretariat of approximately 400 staff, referred to as the Office of the Houses of the Oireachtas.[4] The members of this office are *civil servants of the state*. They are not employed under the same legislation as the departmental civil service (i.e. the Ministers and Secretaries Act, 1924), but instead are employed under the Staff of the Houses of the Oireachtas Act, 1959. They are independent of whatever government may be in power.

The Clerk of the Dáil is the most senior administrator in Leinster House and is the Secretary General of the Office of the Houses of the Oireachtas.[5] He or she is appointed by the Taoiseach, on the joint

---

[4] There are also over 300 political staff working for members of the Houses either in Leinster House or in constituency offices, who are paid through funding provided by the Oireachtas Commission.

[5] The holder of the position is also a member of the Standards in Public Office Commission, Secretary-General of the Houses of the Oireachtas Commission, Registrar of Political Parties and Accounting Officer for the Houses of the Oireachtas.

recommendation of the Ceann Comhairle and the Minister for Finance. The Secretary General is assisted in his/her work by a management committee. The Clerk of the Dáil works closely with the Ceann Comhairle and advises him or her on procedure and precedents. The Clerk opens the sitting of each new Dáil by reading the Presidential Proclamation and the list of members elected for each constituency. He or she also acts as chair until the Ceann Comhairle has been elected.

In 2004, the *Houses of the Oireachtas Commission Act, 2003* came into force. It established the Houses of the Oireachtas Commission. Also, for the first time the Houses have control over their own budget, which is provided in three-year packages, as opposed to an annual vote of money from the Department of Finance. Under the Houses of the Oireachtas Commission Act, 2003, the Commission's 11-person membership is to comprise:

- the Ceann Comhairle
- the Cathaoirleach
- the Clerk of Dáil Éireann
- an appointee of the Minister for Finance
- seven members (Senators and TDs) appointed by the Houses of the Oireachtas.

Since 2000, the Oireachtas has also availed of the services of the *Office of the Parliamentary Legal Adviser*. The main duties of the holder include:

- providing legal advice to the chairpersons of both Houses
- providing legal advice to committees that wish to inquire into matters
- providing legal advice on issues of administrative legal liability assisting with aspects of legislation implementation
- managing the conduct of any legal proceedings involving the Oireachtas
- providing advice on issues of parliamentary privilege, Freedom of Information, ethics legislation, etc.

The holder is not specifically there to offer legal advice to individual TDs, although it may be necessary in some cases.

5

The Oireachtas III:
Seanad Éireann

Seanad Éireann is the Second House or chamber of the Irish parliament. Although often regarded as the more reflective of the two Houses, it has no functions other than debating and amending legislation, and deliberating on motions. In other words, it has no say in the election of the government and cannot dissolve itself. The Seanad was established under the 1922 Irish Free State Constitution, subsequently abolished in 1936, and reconstituted in 1937 with the new Constitution. The Seanad has been credited with improving the quality of legislation over the years, in some cases dramatically so. Largely freed of the constraints imposed by the need for political cohesion, Senators can often bring new and important perspectives to legislation that might otherwise not be heard in the more pressurised Dáil chamber.

Election of the Seanad

A new election to the Seaned must take place within 90 days of the dissolution of the Dáil. The Seanad consists of 60 Senators. Of these:

- 11 are appointed by the Taoiseach at his discretion
- six are elected by graduates of Dublin University and the National University of Ireland
- 43 are elected out of five vocational panels.

The vocational panels are:

- Cultural and Education (5 Senators)
- Agriculture (11)
- Labour (11)

- Industrial and Commercial (9)
- Administrative (7).

Each panel is divided into two sub-panels: one composed of candidates nominated by at least four members of the Oireachtas ('the Oireachtas sub-panel') and one composed of candidates nominated by 98 registered groups representing commerce, trade unions, industry, culture, arts, administration and other professions ('the nominating bodies sub-panel').

To be a nominating body, an organisation must be concerned mainly with or be representative of the interests and services of one or other of the panels; however, a body cannot be registered in respect of more than one panel. Organisations that are mainly profit-making are not eligible for registration, nor are those whose employees are mainly in the employment of the state or local authorities. The Register of Nominating Bodies is reviewed every year by the Clerk of the Seanad.

The Constitution provides that no more than 11 and no fewer than five members can be elected from any one panel.

The electorate for an election of panel members to the Seanad consists of:

- the members of the incoming Dáil
- the members of the outgoing Seanad
- the members of the Councils of Counties and the City/Borough Councils.

Procedures in the Seanad

As with Dáil Éireann, procedures in the Seanad are governed by:

- standing orders
- sessional orders
- *ad hoc* orders and resolutions
- rulings by the Chair
- precedence.

Article 15.10 of the Constitution allows Seanad Éireann the power to make its own rules or standing orders, which establish the method for conducting business in the House. Sessional orders are rules adopted for a parliamentary session only. Of course, they cannot cover every eventuality and the chair of the Seanad may make rulings to supplement the standing orders. The holder of the Chair in the Seanad is called the Cathaoirleach and in his absence, the Leas-Chathaoirleach takes his place. Each sitting of the House is governed by an Order Paper which is prepared under his direction. Motions and amendments are examined individually to ensure that they comply with standing orders and precedents.

Figure 5.1. *Seating arrangements in Seanad Éireann*

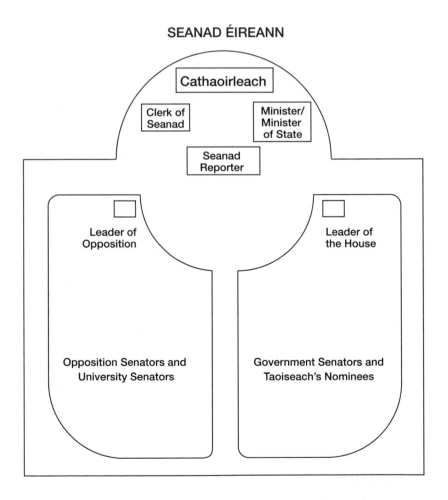

SEANAD ÉIREANN

Cathaoirleach

Clerk of Seanad

Minister/ Minister of State

Seanad Reporter

Leader of Opposition

Leader of the House

Opposition Senators and University Senators

Government Senators and Taoiseach's Nominees

The Cathaoirleach does not normally enter the Chamber until a quorum of 12 deputies is present. The day then opens with the Order of Business when the issues before the Seanad and the time to spend debating them are presented. The Order of Business contains items of government business: any private members' business and any associated proposals that the House needs to make a decision on. Senators often use the Order of Business to raise objections or other issues of concern, but speeches are not allowed. If a member ignores the Chair's rulings, she/he may be 'named', i.e. suspended from the House.

All the issues before the House are published on the Order Paper. Motions for debate must be signed by two Senators to be permitted. Non-government motions are debated for a maximum of two hours, from 6.00 to 8.00 p.m. on Wednesdays.

Raising issues of concern

It is important to note that the Taoiseach and government ministers do not take questions in the Seanad as they do in the Dáil. This is because the Constitution states that the government is responsible to the Dáil only. However, there are methods of raising matters of concern to Senators.

Under Standing Order 28, Senators may raise a matter related to administration of a minister's department on the adjournment of the day's proceedings. Three such matters may be raised on a sitting day, but notice must be given by the previous day at the latest.

Standing Order 30 allows Senators to raise matters of concern on a Thursday. They may be raised via a two-minute statement. The Cathaoirleach may select up to six matters, but they must be submitted no later than 10.00 a.m. on Thursday.

Standing Order 29 allows the Seanad to debate a 'specific and important matter of public interest which has arisen suddenly'. Any member may seek to raise a matter this way by informing the Cathaoirleach in writing not later than 2.30 p.m. on a day when the Seanad meets before noon, and not later than 4.30 p.m. when it meets at noon or after.

Legislation

As noted above, the Seanad's principal role is processing legislation and this takes up the vast bulk of its time. Every sitting day, a Senator will receive:

- a yellow-coloured Order Paper listing all the business before the House that day.
- copies of new and amended Bills and a list of amendments to Bills that are to be taken that day.

When the legislation comes before the House, the minister or minister of state who is sponsoring the legislation will attend the debate to defend the proposed new law. The stages are similar to those in Dáil Éireann (see Chapter 4) and include a committee stage. However, due to the small number of Senators, the committee stage is taken in the House as a whole. Divisions (votes) are taken when a question is put and the response given to the Cathaoirleach challenged. Eight minutes is given between the vote being called and the vote being taken. If a division follows a previous one, then only four minutes is given.

If the Bill originates in the Dáil, the first stage in the Seanad is waived. If it is passed without amendment by the Seanad, it goes to the President to be signed into law. If it is amended by the Seanad, it goes back to the Dáil for consideration.

As in the Dáil, the amendments may be grouped in order to avoid repetition. While broad amendments to the principal of the Bill occur at Second Stage, amendments to the sections, schedules and paragraphs may occur at committee stage. The opposition parties may not move an amendment that may place a charge on the public purse.

At the report (fourth) stage, only amendments that arise out of proceedings in committee are in order. The Bill as a whole is considered, but decisions are made only in respect of amendments and not in respect of individual provisions in the Bill. Only verbal amendments are permitted at the fifth stage.

Interestingly, the Constitution allows the Seanad to petition the President to decline the signing of a Bill until the people have expressed a view on the legislation via a referendum. However, this requires a majority of Senators and at least a third of the Dáil to support the motion.

The Seanad also debates motions on issues that arise and votes on these. Typically, the government will control a majority of seats in the Seanad (this was one of the reasons for allowing the Taoiseach to appoint 11 Senators), and therefore a situation rarely arises whereby the party or parties in government lose a vote.

6

Parliamentary committees

Parliamentary committees represent the most significant institutional development in modern parliaments. In fact, in many legislatures most of the work is conducted in committee format rather than in plenary sessions. While the Dáil and the Seanad continue to be important venues for parliamentarians to debate issues and interrogate government, since their recent emergence in the Oireachtas committees have become essential elements of Irish parliamentary life. In 2006 various committees held more than 500 meetings and produced almost 200 reports. This chapter considers the four different types of parliamentary committees in the Houses of the Oireachtas: the standing, select, special and joint committees.

Standing committees

Standing committees are a permanent feature of the Oireachtas and their re-establishment is automatic after an election. Examples include the following.

- The *Dáil Committee of Public Accounts* examines and reports to the Dáil on the annual Appropriation Accounts (see Chapter 11) and on reports from the Comptroller and Auditor General.
- Both *Dáil and Senate Committees on Members' Interests* are responsible for ensuring that all members comply with the Standards in Ethics in Public Office Act, 1995.

Select committees

Select committees consist of members from one House only and sit to debate legislation at the committee stage (third stage) of legislation. They also consider Estimates of Expenditure from government departments. The select committee's membership will typically be proportional to the make-up of the parent chamber, i.e. a majority of the members will be from the government party or parties. Select committees generally mirror the make-up of government departments, e.g. the Select Committees on Foreign Affairs, Agriculture and Food, Transport.

Special committees

A special committee may be established by either House to consider particular Bills, especially Private Member's Bills, which have passed their second reading and are not being considered in an existing select committee.

Joint committees

Joint committees are composed of members of both chambers and are appointed by an order of each House. Typically, they will be the members of a Dáil select committee who are joined by Senators, and they are involved with the work of the respective government departments. However, joint committees may also be established to consider thematic issues, e.g. climate change. Joint committees do not debate legislation but instead have powers to:

- take oral and written evidence
- print and publish certain material
- invite and accept written submissions
- appoint sub-committees
- draft new legislation
- require a minister or minister of state to discuss policy for which she or he is responsible
- require certain principal office-holders to attend committee meetings to discuss issues for which they are responsible
- engage consultants or specialists
- undertake travel in certain circumstances.

The 30th Dáil (elected in 2007) established 19 joint committees, on:

- Agriculture, Fisheries and Food
- Arts, Sport, Tourism, Community, Rural and Gaeltacht Affairs
- Communications, Energy and Natural Resources
- the Constitution

- Education and Science
- Enterprise, Trade and Employment
- the Environment, Heritage and Local Government
- European Affairs
- European Scrutiny
- Finance and the Public Service
- Foreign Affairs
- Implementation of the Good Friday Agreement
- Health and Children
- Justice, Equality, Defence and Women's Rights
- Social and Family Affairs
- Transport
- Climate Change and Energy Security
- the Constitutional Amendment on Children
- Economic Regulatory Affairs.

Joint committees have both a chairperson and a vice-chairperson; the holders of both positions are remunerated. Joint committees may conduct their work through the establishment of sub-committees. Many of these committees (and sub-committees) produce regular reports, and while there is provision for the reports to be debated in the Dáil and Seanad, it is not obligatory.

As well as those detailed above, some joint committees are also standing committees; for example, the new Joint Committee on Administration has subsumed a number of housekeeping committees, replacing the former Joint Committee on Broadcasting and Parliamentary Information, the Joint House Services Committee, and the Members' Services Committees, and is now responsible for the consideration of the provision of services to members and the Houses generally. Also, there are joint committees that perform special functions. For example, since July 1996, the All-Party Oireachtas Committee on the Constitution has been reviewing the principal features of Bunreacht na hÉireann.

Developing the role of committees

All committees are backed up by a secretariat and each has a clerk. A Committees Directorate co-ordinates the work of the committees. Also, the chairpersons of each committee meet as the Working Group of Committee Chairpersons.

An important piece of legislation governing the work of committees is the *Committees of the Houses of the Oireachtas (Compellability, Privileges and Immunities of Witnesses) Act, 1997*. Under this Act, committees that have been given the power to send for 'persons, papers and records' can, in certain circumstances, come to conclusions and findings of fact in respect of matters under investigation by the committee or a sub-committee appointed by it. The scope of those who can be compelled to attend a committee ranges from the Taoiseach and other members of the government to private citizens. In keeping with the constitutional independence of the President and the judiciary (except in a process involving the removal of a judge from office by virtue of Article 35 of the Constitution), however, they are exempt from being summoned before committees.

Section 15 of the Act precludes public servants from expressing an opinion on the *merits* of any policy of the government or a government minister, or on the *objectives* of any such policy when presenting evidence. Committees are not automatically entitled to the powers of compellability and must apply for them from a sub-committee of the Committee on Procedures and Privileges known as the 'Compellability Committee'.

As can be seen, a major portion of the work of the Houses of the Oireachtas is conducted through the committees. The structure of the existing system provides for a more flexible approach to oversight outside of the more formal platforms of the Dáil and Seanad chambers, as well as more efficient processing of legislation. Furthermore, members of committees avail of the opportunity that the system gives them to engage publicly on many issues. It also offers the opportunity to improve access to the Houses and increase interaction with the public through the hearing of evidence and presentations from witnesses. In this regard, over 1,500 members of the public appeared before committees in 2007. Many groups and individuals avail of the opportunity to engage with parliamentarians in order to influence policy on matters of concern to them. Also, the advent of new technology has allowed for the introduction of *eConsultation*, which seeks to foster a greater public connection to parliament. The programme allows the public to make submissions on matters before the Oireachtas and to contribute to policy consultation and formulation online. Oireachtas committees will increasingly be using mechanisms such as this to seek observations from the public in relation to the development of policy.

7

The government

As noted above, Article 28.2 of the Constitution states that *the executive power of the state shall ... be exercised by or on the authority of the Government*. In other words, the Constitution provides that the government elected by Dáil Éireann is granted executive power, i.e. the power to carry out or 'execute' the will of the public as expressed through parliament. For this reason the government is often referred to as the 'executive'.

There is both a maximalist and a minimalist interpretation of what the executive is. In its broadest sense, the executive may include all aspects of the state apparatus that are charged with implementing the laws and policies of parliament, i.e. the civil service, the local government administration, the police, the state agencies and so on. However, when most commentators speak of the executive they are referring to the Taoiseach and the group of seven to fourteen ministers (normally the maximum number of ministers permissible under the Constitution are appointed) as approved by Dáil Éireann, along with the Chief Whip[6] and ministers of state as appropriate. While the Constitution dictates that all members of the government must be members of either Dáil or Seanad, the Taoiseach, Tánaiste and Minister for Finance must be members of the Dáil only (Article 28.7). Though the term does not appear in the Constitution, the executive is often referred to as the *Cabinet*, and it normally meets on Tuesdays at 10.15 a.m. when the Dáil is sitting and on Wednesdays otherwise. Like the executive of a private business firm, this group decides on (among other things) the key issues of policy and expenditure priorities. It is this latter interpretation of the executive that we will use when we speak of 'the government' in contemporary Ireland.

As noted in Chapter 4, following the election of the Ceann Comhairle, TDs must nominate a TD as Prime Minister, or *Taoiseach*. Candidates are put forward by the main parliamentary parties and the

---

[6] The Chief Whip is normally a minister of state at the Department of the Taoiseach.

candidate who receives a majority of votes is duly nominated. Following this procedure, the Taoiseach must travel to Áras an Uachtaráin (the residence of the President) to be formally appointed by the President, as the Constitution requires. The Taoiseach then returns to the Dáil and proposes his or her Cabinet of Ministers. It is at the discretion of the Taoiseach to decide which members of parliament are nominated to seek the approval of the Dáil for ministerial appointment. As we have seen, in Ireland all ministers must come from the Houses of the Oireachtas (up to two members of Seanad Éireann can be appointed as ministers), a requirement that is not found in many other EU states where ministers may be drawn from wider society.

The Dáil approves the Taoiseach's nominees for ministerial office *en bloc*, i.e. the House does not vote for each minister in turn. When the approval of a majority of the House has been achieved, the ministers make their way to Áras an Uachtaráin to be formally appointed by the President. Also, Article 28.8 provides that 'every minister shall have the right to attend and be heard in each House of the Oireachtas'.Once appointed, a new government decides on the titles and responsibilities of the various ministerial departments. For example, in 2003 the Department of the Environment and Local Government became the Department of the Environment, Heritage and Local Government and in 2007 the Department of Communications, Marine and Natural Resources became the Department of Communications, Energy and Natural Resources.

The business of forming governments has become increasingly complex in recent decades as coalitions of parties are now more common than single-party government. Also, a recent phenomenon has been the development of an agreed 'Programme for Government' by the parties involved in the process of seeking Dáil approval for nomination to office. As detailed below, this sets out the policy priorities for the new administration to guide its work during its term of office, which can last up to five years.

The government's legal adviser – the Attorney General – normally attends Cabinet meetings, as does the Chief Whip and the Secretary General to the Government (who may also be the Secretary General at the Department of the Taoiseach).[7] The government can appoint junior

---

[7] In recent years, a 'super-junior' Minister for Children has also attended Cabinet meetings.

ministers, known as ministers of state, who are delegated functions by their ministers. They help to co-ordinate cross-departmental work and focus on particular issues that may fall between departments. They are not automatically entitled to attend Cabinet meetings, but may be requested to do so if a matter within their remit is to be discussed. The limit on the number of ministers of state that may hold office at any time was increased from 15 to 17 through the enactment of the Ministers and Secretaries (Amendment) Act, 1995, and then to 20 in 2007.

While the government acts under the authority of the Dáil, more often than not parliamentary approval for government decisions comes after they have been made rather than before. Indeed, it would be more correct to say that the executive has become the major agent in the formulation of policies and legislation and that, to a great extent, parliament reacts to and gives its imprimatur to its proposals. The ever-expanding role of the state demands that the Cabinet of Ministers be in a position to make and agree important policy decisions when they meet. The government must also be proactive rather than reactive, and consequently it plays a decisive role in policy formulation. In Cabinet, therefore, differences are reconciled (as far as possible) and a consensus is reached on such issues as:

- the allocation of state resources
- approving legislation to go before parliament for debate
- co-ordinating national policy in line with financial, EU and other constraints.

The 1991 Local Government Act stated that ministers and ministers of state could not also hold a seat on a local authority. This was reaffirmed by the 2001 Local Government Act, which ended the practice of any member of the Oireachtas holding a mandate at local level.

As of 2003, a code of conduct applies to all those who hold public office,[8] including:

- the Taoiseach
- the Tánaiste
- a minister

---

[8] The code also applies to the Chair and Deputy Chair of Dáil Éireann and Seanad Éireann.

- a minister of state
- an Attorney General who is a member of Dáil Éireann or Seanad Éireann.

The code establishes standards with respect to donations, gifts, constituency matters and other areas where the potential for abuse of public office exists. It is informed by the Ethics in Public Office Act, 1995 and the Standards in Public Office Act, 2001, which set out the requirements concerning disclosure to which office-holders must adhere.

The government employs a Government Information Service (GIS) to provide information on government policy to the public and to promote a co-ordinated approach to media matters across government departments. This service works closely with the Government Press Office in co-ordinating the media aspects of state visits and major government events, and issues details weekly on ministerial engagements. Since 1997 there has been a Communications Unit which provides a media information service for the government and its departments. As the media has developed its investigative and oversight roles in recent years, the desire of politicians to be able to use the media effectively to get their message across has increased.

In order that central government function effectively, there are two key doctrines that govern the business of Cabinet – collective responsibility and ministerial responsibility.

Collective responsibility

Article 28.4 of the Constitution states that:

> The Government shall be responsible to Dáil Éireann. The Government shall meet and act as a collective authority, and shall be collectively responsible for the Departments of State administered by the members of the Government.

Collective responsibility implies that all members of the executive share culpability for the policies of the government and therefore provide Dáil Éireann with the means of holding the whole government accountable. Each minister is given a portfolio that bestows on him/her responsibility for a specific department. In addition to having responsibility for their own departments, government ministers are collectively responsible for all departments. The doctrine of collective responsibility normally ensures that ministers make their colleagues aware of their plans before they make them public. If a minister is absent or indisposed for a given time, his/her responsibilities can be temporarily assigned to another minister. The Tánaiste acts in place of the Taoiseach during his or her absence.

Cabinet confidentiality

Matters discussed at meetings of the government are confidential. The National Archives Act, 1986 placed a 30-year release rule on Cabinet *discussions* (i.e. the deliberations leading to decisions). The Freedom of Information Act, 1997 allowed access to Cabinet *records* (i.e. the principal decisions taken) after five years. This was extended to 10 years in 2003 with the Freedom of Information (Amendment) Act.

Following a referendum on the issue of Cabinet confidentiality in 1997, in certain circumstances the High Court can decide that government discussions may be released. Of course, after Cabinet meetings the Taoiseach or a senior member of the government may inform the media about decisions taken, but the content of discussions is not normally divulged. Since 1998, facilities have been provided in government departments for former ministers and ministers of state to store documents and records from their time in office.

Ministerial responsibility

The other key doctrine of government – ministerial responsibility – is arguably the keystone of government accountability. Under the 1924 Ministers and Secretaries Act, *the Oireachtas has no direct constitutional linkage with the civil service*. Instead, civil servants are accountable to their minister, who has been granted executive power by the Oireachtas.[9] The principal function of this Act was to provide a legal basis for the minister to be the source of authority in a government department.[10] However, it also provided that the minister in charge of a

---

[9] The exception to this is the requirement of Secretaries-General in their capacity as 'accounting officers' to appear before the Committee of Public Accounts to answer questions concerning their departmental budget.

department would legally be considered a 'corporation sole', i.e. he or she could sign contracts, buy and sell land, and sue or be sued as a corporate entity rather than as an individual. While ministerial responsibility primarily provides for the responsibility of ministers for the work of their departments, it also enables parliament to focus on the work of a particular minister rather than censuring the whole government.

Of course, because of collective responsibility, the departmental minister cannot have a policy that diverges from that of Cabinet. It follows that once Cabinet has made a decision, the actions and policy statements of departmental civil servants must conform to those of the minister and the government as a whole. For these reasons, ministerial responsibility and collective responsibility have been the defining features of Westminster-type parliamentary systems and are crucial elements in the chain of accountability from the public administration to the people.

Cabinet sub-committees

Just as we have seen how parliament increasingly relies on committees to conduct its work, so too have sub-units emerged at Cabinet level. Cabinet sub-committees (also known simply as Cabinet committees) are increasingly common in modern Irish government, particularly with the recognition of the need for cross-departmental work in many areas. Some Cabinet sub-committees have existed for a long period, e.g. the former Cabinet Sub-Committee on Northern Ireland and Security; others are created on a more *ad hoc* basis, e.g. the Cabinet Sub-Committee on Asylum and Immigration Issues, Cabinet Sub-Committee on Social Inclusion and Cabinet Sub-Committee on Decentralisation. In February 2005, in response to the crisis over illegal deductions from pensions and other state payments belonging to nursing home residents by the state, the government set up a Cabinet sub-committee consisting of the Taoiseach, the Tanaiste (who was then also the Minister for Health), the Minister for Finance and the Attorney General. When a government leaves office, the sub-committees are terminated and must be re-created by an incoming administration. The

---

[10] The 1997 Public Service Management Act, however, allowed for devolution of authority for certain functions from ministers to senior civil servants (see Chapter 8).

new government appointed in April 2007 established six Cabinet sub-committees, with the Taoiseach a member of each.[11] The sub-committees do not have decision-making power but instead submit policy proposals to the full Cabinet by way of a memorandum for government. The frequency of Cabinet sub-committee meetings varies and the discussions also benefit from Cabinet confidentiality.

The Taoiseach

As the Head of Government, the Taoiseach has a leadership and co-ordination role in respect of the work of all government departments. He chairs government meetings and directs their agenda. Indeed, any issue to be submitted for a government meeting must first receive his or her permission. As the chief policy-maker, the Taoiseach is responsible for the direction of government policy. He or she is constitutionally required to keep the President informed on international and domestic policy matters, but how often this occurs is at the discretion of the Taoiseach. As noted above, he or she also has considerable powers of nomination and appointment.

The Taoiseach can reshuffle ministers during the government's term of office; titles and functions of departments can also be changed by the government. If the Taoiseach resigns from office, ministers are also deemed to have resigned; however, they carry on their duties until their successors are appointed. Since the office of Taoiseach was created in 1937, 12 persons have held the position (Table 7.1).

The Department of the Taoiseach provides back-up assistance to the Taoiseach in regard to the operation of the government system. Within the department, the Government Secretariat assists the Taoiseach with business related to Cabinet meetings. Constitutional and legal advice is provided by the Attorney General (see below). Also, in recent years, the office-holder has had programme managers and advisers who provide informed advice on policy issues. Like all ministers, the Taoiseach also has a private office.

---

[11] These committees were European Affairs, Health, Climate Change and Energy Security, Housing, Infrastructure and Public-Private Partnerships, Social Inclusion, Children and Integration, and Science, Technology and Innovation.

Table 7.1. *List of Taoisigh*

Since the first Dáil met in January 1919, 15 men have held a position equivalent to Prime Minister in Ireland. Under the 1922 Constitution, the office was referred to as the President of the Executive Council, and the 1937 Constitution changed the title to *Taoiseach*. The following persons have held these positions:

Cathal Brugha (January 1919–April 1919)
Eamonn de Valera (April 1919–August 1921)
Arthur Griffith (January 1921–September 1922)
Michael Collins (January 1922–August 1922)
W.T. Cosgrave (August 1922–March 1932)
Éamon de Valera (March 1932–February 1948)
John A. Costello (February 1948–June 1951)
Éamon de Valera (June 1951–June 1954)
John A. Costello (June 1954–March 1957)
Éamon de Valera (March 1957–June 1959)
Sean F. Lemass (June 1959–November 1966)
Jack Lynch (November 1966–March 1973)
Liam Cosgrave (March 1973–June 1977)
Jack Lynch (July 1977–December 1979)
Charles J. Haughey (December 1979–June 1981)
Garret FitzGerald (June 1981–January 1982)
Charles J. Haughey (March 1982–December 1982)
Garret FitzGerald (December 1982–March 1987)
Charles J. Haughey (March 1987–February 1992)
Albert Reynolds (February 1992–December 1994)
John Bruton (December 1994–June 1997)
Bertie Ahern (June 1997–May 2008)
Brian Cowen (May 2008 to date)

The Government Secretariat

This group of officials is headed by the Secretary General to the Government. There is also an Assistant Secretary to the Government. The Government Secretariat co-ordinates all the proposed business and prepares the agenda (normally on the previous Friday) for each meeting of the government, which takes place the following week. It operates under a set of detailed procedures in a booklet called the *Cabinet Handbook*. As noted below, every item of business put before the Cabinet must be the subject of a memorandum from the minister concerned, and it must clearly state the background, the arguments for and against the solution being put forward, cost and staffing implications, and the views of other ministers. Memoranda must reach the secretary to the government not later than three days before they are to be considered.

The Secretary General to the Government is the only official who attends government meetings. The Secretary General takes the notes and immediately after each meeting he transmits the decisions relating to particular departments to the private secretaries of the ministers concerned, so that they may be acted on departmentally. The Secretariat also sends Bills to the President for signature. Minutes taken by the Secretary General record decisions taken.

The positions of Secretary General to the Government and Secretary General of the Department of the Taoiseach used to be separate roles, but they are now vested in the one office. The Taoiseach also has the assistance of a Government Press Secretary and the Government Press Office.

Legislative Proposals and Memoranda to Cabinet

Policy formulation usually comes from senior civil servants in a department who advise their minister on the best course of action to take. The minister then proposes the policy to Cabinet by sending a *memorandum* in advance of the Cabinet meeting and making a short presentation to the Cabinet.

In terms of legislation, the first stage in the process involves the minister seeking the approval of his Cabinet colleagues for the drafting of a Bill by way of a Memorandum to Government. The Office of the Attorney General is also notified of this intention, particularly if a question of constitutionality arises. If such approval is forthcoming, the minister's department prepares the 'Heads' of the Bill, which sets out the key sections of the legislation along with explanatory notes and a regulatory impact analysis (RIA – see Chapter 8). These documents, known as the General Scheme of the Bill, are then forwarded to the other departments, which prepare their responses, if any, for the next Cabinet meeting. Oireachtas committees may also be consulted for their views. The Bill may or may not be rejected by Cabinet at this stage.

If the Cabinet approves the general scheme of a Bill, a formal request is sent to the Attorney General's Office accompanied by a copy of the Cabinet decision for drafting. The request to the Attorney

General's Office is that the Bill be drafted by the Office of Parliamentary Counsel (OPC). When the request for drafting is received in the OPC, it is sent to the 'group' dealing with the department sponsoring the Bill and the group leader will assign the drafting of the Bill to a drafter (parliamentary counsel). The OPC is divided into three groups, each of which deals with a certain number of departments assigned to it.

The assigned drafter then proceeds to draft the Bill on the lines of the instructions in the Heads and consults with the department concerned. A lot of consultation with departments may be done by telephone, but it is usual for there to be a number of meetings as well. Certain issues where legal or drafting points arise will be conducted through formal correspondence, where the drafter considers this is necessary. The drafter can consult with an advisory counsel (a member of the advisory side of the Attorney General's Office) when legal or constitutional issues arise. While the policy behind a proposed Bill should be worked out at the Heads of Bill stage, subsidiary matters frequently arise as a Bill is being drafted which require policy decisions by the department.

The time it takes to draft a Bill depends on its complexity, its urgency and the quality of the instructions and the competence and overall workload of the instructing officials. Legislation in an emergency situation can be drafted in a very short time. When the drafting of a Bill is complete, the drafter has each page of the Bill stamped with the OPC stamp. The department, when satisfied that it reflects what is required, circulates a draft Memorandum to Government to relevant departments for their observations.

In due course, the minister sponsoring the legislation brings the now fully detailed draft Bill to Cabinet for approval and a decision to publish. If Cabinet approves the Bill and agrees to its initiation for debate and scrutiny in either the Dáil or Seanad, a certified copy is sent to the Bills Office in the Oireachtas. The Bill is then initiated on a specified date into either the Dáil (printed on green paper) or the Seanad (printed on yellow paper). The initiation by publication is the first stage of the Bill as described in Chaper 4.

Certificate of Urgency
The main Cabinet agenda is normally compiled on the Friday before the next scheduled meeting, with a deadline of 12 noon for the submission of items. However, if a matter is deemed to be sufficiently important, and has missed the normal Friday submission deadline, a

Certificate of Urgency may be issued by the relevant minister (or in his/her absence a senior civil servant not below Assistant Secretary level) to have it so included. The Certificate of Urgency must be accompanied by a statement explaining why it was not submitted in the normal manner.

Memorandum for the Information of Government

Formerly known as an *Aide-Mémoire*, the purpose of a Memorandum for the Information of Government is to bring to the government's attention a matter that may be of importance but does not require any policy decision. It is circulated to ministers via an internal system known as e-Cabinet.

Submitting memoranda to government

There are very strict rules governing the drafting of memoranda to government.[12] In summary, in order to be accepted, memoranda must:

- be clearly worded
- prominently indicate the decision being sought
- provide a summary of expected costs
- deal adequately with observations made by other ministers
- include a timeframe for implementation of the decision, if achieved
- include, where appropriate, a regulatory impact analysis (see Chapter 8)
- indicate the impact of the proposal on North–South and East–West relations, employment, gender equality, poverty and social exclusion, costs to industry, and rural communities.

Every draft memorandum involving policy proposals is forwarded to the Departments of the Taoiseach and Finance via e-Cabinet (as well as the offices of the leaders of all parties in the case of a coalition government). If there are substantive constitutional or legal dimensions, the Attorney General should receive a copy. A copy should also be sent to departments that may be affected by the proposal. Departments are normally expected to respond within two weeks, or three weeks for legislative proposals.

---

[12] Full details are available online at www.taoiseach.gov.ie

Green Papers and White Papers

In order to initiate a public debate and elicit views on a subject, governments often publish a Green Paper. While a Green Paper may lead to a change in the law, it is not a commitment to legislation but rather represents the government's thinking on an issue and initiates a period of consultation. Within the EU, the Commission (see Chapter 19) may produce Green Papers for similar reasons.

A White Paper is a more robust document, and is usually a precursor to legislation. A White Paper normally follows a Green Paper and is a more detailed series of proposals that represent government thinking and intentions on a particular issue or policy. While White Papers also stimulate debate, they are less likely to be amended than Green Papers.

The Attorney General

The Office of the Attorney General was created under the 1924 Ministers and Secretaries Act (section 6). It achieved constitutional status in 1937 under Article 30, which reads as follows.

1. There shall be an Attorney General who shall be the adviser of the Government in matters of law and legal opinion, and shall exercise and perform all such powers, functions and duties as are conferred or imposed on him by this Constitution or by law.
2. The Attorney General shall be appointed by the President on the nomination of the Taoiseach.
3. All crimes and offences prosecuted in any court constituted under Article 34 of this Constitution other than a court of summary jurisdiction shall be prosecuted in the name of the People and at the suit of the Attorney General or some other person authorised in accordance with law to act for that purpose.
4. The Attorney General shall not be a member of the Government.

Though not technically a member of the government, he or she traditionally attends Cabinet meetings and retires when the government falls. The Attorney General therefore has a very close working relationship with the Taoiseach of the day, who nominates him or her. As noted above, on behalf of the government the Attorney General scrutinises (from a constitutional and legal point of view) all draft legislation that any government department proposes to bring before the Oireachtas. Drafting of primary legislation is carried out by an office within the Attorney General's office known as the *Office of Parliamentary Counsel to the Government*. Another section of the Attorney General's office contains a number of *Advisory Counsel* who assist the Attorney General, provide advice to departments on a broad range of legal issues, and assist in matters of civil litigation and the development of legislation. The Chief State Solicitor's office (see Chapter 15) is also a constituent part of the Office of the Attorney General.

The Attorney General's functions include:

- *representing the public* in all legal proceedings for the enforcement of law in Ireland and the assertion or protection of public rights
- *acting as lawyer for the state* in virtually all civil litigation in which the state or its officers are official parties
- *giving legal advice* on matters that are submitted by government departments and offices and drafting necessary accompanying legal documents
- *providing a solicitor service in all civil courts* and tribunals in which the state, any state authority or the Attorney General is involved.

The Attorney General also advises the government on international agreements. As with ministers, the Attorney General's tenure in office can be terminated by the President if the Taoiseach so advises.

The Office of the Attorney General is also responsible for the Statute Law Revision Project, which seeks to repeal legislation that existed pre-Independence and serves no useful purpose today, as well as to consolidate other legislation. To date, over 3,400 Acts have been repealed, thus making the Irish Statute Book more accessible for all.

The Programme for Government

Since 1989, all Irish governments have been coalitions, i.e. they have consisted of more than one political party. Every recent government has begun its work by producing a 'Programme for Government' that sets out high-level goals which it wishes to achieve in the course of its lifetime (a maximum of five years). These programmes provide the basis for all government work, and normally take cognisance of other existing national strategies. For example, the government elected in 2007 contained three political parties (Fianna Fáil, the Progressive Democrats and the Green Party); its Programme for Government (agreed before the election of the new Taoiseach and ministers by the Dáil) ran to 86 pages and covered a very broad range of policy areas. Also, the programme committed the new government to upholding the work set out in the *National Development Plan 2007–13* and the social partnership agreement *Towards 2016*.

In order to ensure that the objectives of the programme are being met, it has become standard practice for ministers and their senior civil servants to meet at least once annually with the Taoiseach and his equivalent staff to review progress in each department against the Programme for Government. With every new government (or the appointment of a new minister) each department is required to develop a three-year strategic work plan that will also reflect the Programme for Government's objectives.

Special advisers/Programme managers

With the advent of Programmes for Government, it is increasingly common for ministers to appoint non-elected 'programme managers' to ensure the coherence of policy within their department and across government. The first such positions were created during the 1993/4 government, where the managers were appointed to co-ordinate and monitor the progress of the Programme of Government agreed between the Labour Party and Fianna Fáil. Some of these managers were civil servants but others were appointed from outside the civil service. The managers met weekly and reported regularly to their ministers; their employment lasted as long as that of the minister. Programme managers still form part of Irish government today.

As well as the managers, ministers may appoint personal 'special advisers' to assist them, who are also not civil servants. The government must approve the appointments, which are not advertised publicly. Many of these appointees will have expertise in particular areas of government, e.g. economics, social development, and they are usually supporters of the governing party or parties. Since the early 1980s, almost all ministers have appointed special advisers.

These appointments bear a resemblance to the practice in the larger states of the EU, where members of the government each have a *cabinet* of advisers, who work closely with the minister on his policy programme. No equivalent official cabinet-type system exists in Ireland. The Public Service Management Act, 1997 made legislative provision for the appointment of special advisers. It states that:

(2) A Special Adviser to a Minister or to a Minister of State, as the case may be, shall –

    (*a*) assist the Minister or the Minister of State, as the case may be, by –
        (i) providing advice,
        (ii) monitoring, facilitating and securing the achievement of Government objectives that relate to the Department, as requested by the Minister or the Minister of State, as the case may be, and
        (iii) performing such other functions as may be directed by the Minister or the Minister of State, as the case may be, that are not otherwise provided for in this Act and do not involve the exercise of any specific powers conferred on the Minister or the Minister of State, as the case may be, or any other office holder by or under any other Act, and
    (*b*) be accountable to the Minister or the Minister of State, as the case may be, in the performance of those functions.

While special advisers appear to be an enduring feature of government, in May 2008 the new Taoiseach Brian Cowen decided that they could no longer attend Cabinet sub-committee meetings, a practice that had emerged in recent years. Instead, such meetings would in future consist of ministers, ministers of state and Secretaries General only.

8

The civil service

Previous chapters on the Oireachtas and the government identified how they were *political* institutions – political parties competed to control them through elections. However, implementation of the many decisions taken in these institutions requires a system of *public administration* (or bureaucracy) that has the capacity to deal with competing pressures and demands not only from politics, but also from the public and the economy. The Irish public administration is a large and complex organisation with many elements, as later chapters detail. We begin here by considering the part of the administration that works closest to government – the civil service.

What is the civil service?

Section 1 of the Civil Service Regulation Act 1956 stated that '"the Civil Service" means the Civil Service of the Government and the Civil Service of the State'. We have noted above that the Houses of the Oireachtas are served by civil servants *of the state*. Reflecting the separation of powers, the civil service of the *government* comprises those individuals or civil servants who work within government departments headed by a minister, as well as a number of related offices established to carry out specific functions. These offices include:

- Office of the Attorney General
- Revenue Commissioners
- Office of the Appeal Commissioners
- Office of Public Works
- Central Statistics Office
- Office of the Chief Science Adviser to the Government
- Office of the Comptroller and Auditor General
- Director of Public Prosecutions
- Courts Service of Ireland.

Chapter 9 will consider in more detail the growing number of state bodies or agencies that now work with departments. It suffices here to note that all civil servants are employed by the Minister for Finance by virtue of the 1924 Ministers and Secretaries Act, which states in Section 2(3) that:

> The terms and conditions of appointment of all officers and servants appointed by any Minister shall be prescribed by the Minister for Finance and [they] shall be paid out of moneys provided by the Oireachtas.

The origins of the Irish civil service

At the height of the industrial revolution in mid-nineteenth-century Britain, the responsibilities of government began to accumulate rapidly, and as a consequence the number of people employed in the administrative system expanded. In 1854 – following a request by the Chancellor of the Exchequer in London, William Gladstone – two Treasury officials, Northcote and Trevelyan, produced a brief report on the future of the Civil Service. Their main recommendations were that:

- civil servants should be recruited by open competitive examination, with the examinations conducted by an independent central board
- promotion should be on merit rather than seniority, thus ending the practice of patronage.

There was initial reluctance to accept these reforms, and it was not until Gladstone became Prime Minister in 1868 that the proposals made an impact.

Upon independence in 1922, the Irish Free State government did not fundamentally depart from this system of impartial public administration that it had inherited. Indeed, the British civil service was regarded as the most effective in the world at that time, having undergone considerable reorganisation after the First World War. Instead, control of the Irish civil service, which had previously been exercised by the Treasury, was eventually assumed by the *Minister for Finance* (with the exception of the period 1973–87, when it was the responsibility of the Minister for Public Service).

The 1924 Ministers and Secretaries Act also provided for the formal structure of the service. It created 11 departments of state and distributed activities among them; as noted above, it also provided the legal basis for the mechanics and organisation of the civil service through the definition of ministerial responsibility. Civil servants enjoyed security of tenure. The Civil Service Regulation Acts, 1923, 1924 and 1926 governed recruitment to and regulation of the civil service. The statutory position with regard to recruitment and regulation was brought up to date by the enactment of the Civil Service Commissioners Act, 1956 and the Civil Service Regulation Act, 1956. As the role of the state has expanded in more recent decades, so too has the size of the service, and in recent years many civil servants have found themselves working for agencies under the aegis of government departments (see Chapter 9).

Civil service values

Just as there are different types of parliament and government, there are different types of civil service. In some states, the need for loyalty has meant that senior civil servants are avowedly partisan and are appointed by politicians who want to ensure that the bureaucracy shares their belief in their decisions. Other systems, such as that of the UK and Ireland, are founded on the principle of impartiality and are avowedly non-political. This is manifest in the requirement that senior civil servants in both these states cannot be members of political parties or run for political office while employed by the state. The civil service is therefore politically neutral and, as in many other jurisdictions, is not recognised in the Constitution.

The work of the civil service is informed by certain key values, many of which operate throughout the Irish public service. These include honesty, impartiality, equity, integrity, fairness, probity and political neutrality.[13] Civil servants are also required to adhere to the stipulations of the Official Secrets Act, which all new recruits must sign. This Act seeks to prevent improper disclosure of information gained in the course of civil servants' work, such as issues concerning national security or commercial activity by the state. However, recent Freedom of Information legislation provides for greater access to general information by the public (see below).

---

[13] For more on civil service values, see the Civil Service Code of Standards and Behaviour, available at www.sipo.gov.ie/en/CodesofConduct/CivilServants

The work of the civil service

The civil service administers a vast range of policy areas, from health to foreign policy, agriculture to defence. The taxpayer funds the civil service and is entitled to know how it works and how it reaches its decisions. There is therefore an onus on the civil service to be impartial in its dealings with all members of the public and to be able to demonstrate this. We therefore find a higher commitment to record-keeping than might be typical in other parts of the workforce.

Traditionally, the civil service has been charged with two main tasks – to assist members of the government in making policy; and to carry out policy decisions. In recent years, the civil service has increasingly been tasked with other duties, such as regulating not only the distribution of resources but also the manner in which government policies are implemented. In this respect, the civil service may be considered part of the executive insofar as it is charged with carrying out the will of the government as approved by parliament. It does not have the final say in public policy and works subject to the authority of government, which is ultimately responsible to the people.

Taken as a whole, the departments of government are charged with the essential responsibilities of any modern democratic state, i.e.:

* administration
* justice
* the creation and maintenance of infrastructure
* the welfare of citizens
* promotion of enterprise
* national security.

In deciding how best to perform these duties within a limited budget, choices have to be made by politicians elected to power. However, the point where politics ends and administration begins is hard to identify, and many would argue that they are inseparable. Politics is where public opinion is formed, social interests are debated and confront each other, political parties debate and decisions are taken. Public administration is portrayed as a less volatile environment with no partisan passions, devoted to advisory, clerical and technical work. In reality the two are closely interlinked – the work of government departments is wholly dependent on the state. The state's performance is constrained by the capacities of its administrative system.

Each element of the public administration specialises in a specific task and the combination of their tasks achieves the purposes of the state.

There are several theories as to how policy emerges. Technically the Cabinet decides on policy, parliament approves it, and the civil service sees that it is implemented. In reality, the civil service clearly has a strong advisory role in shaping policies the minister puts to government and parliament. The strength of civil service influence will vary from minister to minister and from case to case. In any event, the civil service remains an integral part of the state's machinery and worthy of detailed study.

As of 2007, there are 15 government departments including the Department of the Taoiseach (Prime Minister). Most government departments also have certain state agencies within their remit (see Chapter 9). For example, the Data Protection Commissioner is under the aegis of the Department of Justice, Equality and Law Reform. The National Roads Authority reports to the Department of Transport and the Broadcasting Commission of Ireland is mainly funded by the Department of Communications, Energy and Natural Resources.

As of 2008, the departments are as follows (in alphabetical order):

- Agriculture, Fisheries and Food
- Arts, Sport and Tourism
- Communications, Energy and Natural Resources
- Community, Rural and Gaeltacht Affairs
- Defence
- Education and Science
- Enterprise, Trade and Employment
- Environment, Heritage and Local Government
- Finance
- Foreign Affairs
- Health and Children
- Justice, Equality and Law Reform
- Social and Family Affairs
- Taoiseach
- Transport.

Internal structures and grading

Approximately 38,000 people are employed in the civil service, representing less than 2% of the labour force. There are three principal career structures in the civil service, as follows.

1. Those employed in the general civil service and who engage in the work of civil service departments and offices, from clerical duties to management. This cohort is the principal focus of this chapter.
2. Those employed in other parts of the public administration, such as the Houses of the Oireachtas or the Office of the Ombudsman.
3. Those involved in technical or specialist work and who provide particular skill, e.g. auditors, architects, solicitors.

These three categories consist of myriad positions and grades, some of which contain only one person, e.g. the Comptroller and Auditor General; others consist of many people. Within the general service, responsibility in a government department moves along nine principal grades, represented hierarchically in Figure 8.1.

Figure 8.1. *Principal civil service grades*

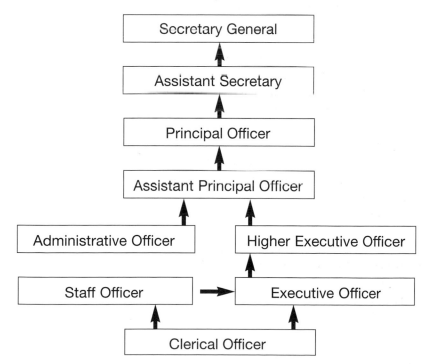

It is important to note that those in the general service grades from Assistant Principal upwards constitute what is sometimes referred to as the *Higher Civil Service.* They are charged with providing advice and options to ministers, examining proposals for change and managing large projects.

A report[14] in 2004 categorised the grades as follows.

- *Senior management:* Secretary General, Deputy Secretary,[15] Assistant Secretary
- *Management:* Principal Officer, Assistant Principal
- *Executive:* Higher Executive Officer, Administrative Officer, Executive Officer
- *Administrative support:* Staff Officer, Clerical Officer
- *Non-clerical support:* Services Officer, Services Attendant
- *Technical/Professional:* technical and professional grades

Given its close relationship to government, it is worth considering the position of Secretary General in more detail here, as well as including a brief note on the work of the other grades.

Secretaries General

Formerly known as 'Secretaries', Secretaries General are the most senior civil servants, with normally one Secretary General heading up each department.[16] A Secretary General may hold his or her post for an initial seven years and their primary role is to manage their department.

With the exceptions noted above, Secretaries General are normally selected by the Top Level Appointments Committee (TLAC – see below). The committee selects candidates based on their management skills, leadership qualities and ability to formulate acceptable policies that satisfy political and economic constraints.

Along with Assistant Secretaries and Principals, they are the most influential members of the bureaucracy. Their primary functions are management, policy appraisal, policy formulation and often policy

---

14 Mercer Human Resource Consulting (2004) *Evaluation of the PMDS for the Civil Service.* Department of the Taoiseach.

15 The position of Deputy Secretary exists in a small number of departments.

16 Within a department, it is possible to have a second Secretary General with responsibility for a particular area of concern. For example, within the Department of Finance there is a position of Secretary General for Public Service Management and Development.

implementation. In recent years it has become common practice for Secretaries General to meet as a group after Cabinet meetings. Each Secretary General has a close relationship with his or her minister, though this has proved difficult to define.

A recent attempt to clarify the role of the Secretary General was made in the report of a high-level Working Group on the Accountability of Secretaries-General and Accounting Officers, established by the government in 2000. Known as the Mullarkey Report (after its chairman), the report considered the dual role played by Secretaries General as senior civil servants and as financial watchdogs or 'Accounting Officers' for their respective departments. In their role as Accounting Officers, Secretaries General appear before the Committee of Public Accounts in their personal capacity rather than as a representative of their minister.

The Mullarkey Report demonstrates the complexities of the dual role. Commenting on the relationship between the minister and the Secretary General, the report noted the following.

The working relationship between the Secretary General and the Minister who is in charge of the Department is a key factor in the effective administration of Government Departments. The constitutional, legislative and administrative framework within which Departments operate necessitates that civil servants operating under the authority of the Minister implement Government policy set by the Minister. Within the statutory framework, Secretaries General have considerable authority within Departments of State subject to the overriding authority of the Minister. They have a pivotal role in providing independent advice to the Minister and in managing the interface between the Department and the Minister. In their capacity as managers of Departments they have a responsibility to ensure that the systems and procedures are in place to enable it to perform its functions within the resources available and to enable the Minister to answer for the performance of those functions to the Dáil. This requires the Minister to place trust and confidence in the Secretary General. The distinctive relationship of trust and confidence between the Minister and the Secretary General is crucial to the effective administration of Departments of State and places the Secretary General in a different position to other civil servants. The relationship extends beyond the Minister and requires the Government as a whole to place confidence in the Secretary General.

As the *heads of government departments*, Secretaries General have authority for:

- managing the organisation to implement and monitor policy and to achieve agreed outputs
- advising on policy
- ensuring that the appropriate arrangements are in place to respond effectively to cross-departmental issues
- appointments and discipline.

For this work they are accountable in different ways and in varying degrees to the government , their minister (or minister(s) of state where they exist), Oireachtas committees and the public.

The Mullarkey Report states that as *Accounting Officers*, Secretaries General have authority for the following.

- Ensuring that all relevant financial considerations are taken into account and, where necessary, brought to the attention of the minister where they concern the preparation and implementation of policy proposals relating to income or expenditure for which s/he is Accounting Officer.
- Economy and efficiency in the administration of the department including having adequate financial management systems in place.
- The adequacy of arrangements within the department to ensure the correctness of all payments; and the efficient recovery and bringing to account of all receipts connected with the Vote, or with any fund for which the department is responsible; and ensuring that Finance sanction for expenditure has been obtained.
- Responsibilities in respect of internal audit with a view to ensuring that s/he is getting the desired quality of assurance in relation to the department's internal control system.
- Responsibilities in respect of grants-in-aid to outside agencies.
- The Accounting Officer also has responsibilities for ensuring that there is a clear framework for control and accountability of public funds in bodies operating under the aegis of the department.

In their role as Accounting Officers, Secretaries General are answerable to the Committee of Public Accounts, which in turn reports to the Dáil, for the proper expenditure of money voted by the Dáil for which they have responsibility. Traditionally, the civil service head of the department was appointed Accounting Officer because she or he alone had sufficient authority within the department to discharge the responsibilities attaching to the role. The role of Accounting Officer has long been regarded as one of the linchpins in the financial administration of the state, particularly in relation to the accountability for moneys voted by the Oireachtas. The role of Accounting Officer is a long-standing feature of financial administration in the Irish civil service which predates the foundation of the state.

Accounting Officers have wide-ranging responsibilities for financial management. In particular they are responsible for the safeguarding of public funds and property under their control and for the regularity and propriety of transactions in the Appropriation Accounts (see Chapter 11) bearing their signature as well as any other account, subject to audit by the Comptroller and Auditor General, that they or the department are required to prepare under statute. Arising from changes in the scope of public audit in recent years, the Accounting Officer also has responsibilities for value for money in the terms provided for in the Comptroller and Auditor General (Amendment) Act, 1993.

Assistant Secretary

A grade below the Secretary General is the Assistant Secretary (or Deputy Secretary). He or she performs many duties that are similar to those of Principals, but they have a higher level of responsibility and usually a wider remit. Assistant Secretaries meet regularly with ministers.

Principal and Assistant Principal Officers

Principal Officers (POs) have responsibility for planning, management and overview of policy in large sections of their department. In their work, they may be supported by Assistant Principal Officers (APOs), who assume responsibility for certain elements of this work.

Administrative Officer

Administrative Officers (AOs) are involved with policy formulation for a wide range of government areas through a combination of critical analysis, research and policy drafting. AOs frequently work closely with HEOs (see below) and are often required to prepare briefing material for ministers.

Executive Officers and Higher Executive Officers
The position of Executive Officer (EO) is akin to that of a trainee manager, and that of Higher Executive Officer (HEO) to a manager. Executive Officers are engaged in analysis, decision-making, planning and organising people and resources. For this reason, the EO and HEO grades are often referred to as middle management.

Clerical Officer
Clerical Officers are key to the successful operation of the civil service and make up over half of the general service grades. They are concerned with recording information, checking accounts, filing, answering telephones and other essential administrative duties.

As noted above, various departments will also have specialist or technical staff according to the type of work they are involved with. For example, the Department of the Environment, Heritage and Local Government will have several engineers and architects in its ranks. The Department of Agriculture and Food will employ several vets on a full-time basis. Other technical staff include:

- planners
- marine biologists
- accountants/auditors
- medical consultants
- psychologists
- nursing staff
- legal staff – solicitors, barristers, law clerks
- paramedical staff – dental surgeons,
- environmental health officers, pharmacists,
- Community Welfare Officers.

The Management Advisory Committee
An important development for all civil service departments has been the establishment of a Management Advisory Committee (MAC). It consists of the Secretary General and the senior management team (usually Assistant Secretaries) in the department and normally considers a range of matters from policy to in-house management. However, ministers and ministers of state may also attend, as may the minister's special adviser(s), though the practice varies. While no uniform policy exists across departments concerning the frequency of such meetings, the MAC tends to meet weekly.

The role of the MAC is to link the department's corporate strategy and objectives to its day-to-day operations, as well as ensuring that strategy formulation is informed by operating realities. The MAC also plays a pivotal role in relation to internal and external communications and, when ministers and/or their advisers attend, provides an avenue for exchange of information between political and administrative spheres.

Recruitment

In order to maintain the impartial nature of the public administration in post-Civil War Ireland, the Civil Service Commission (and Local Appointments Commission) was established in 1926. It ensured that appointments to the bureaucracy would be independent of partisan politics. The commission was based in Dublin and was involved solely in recruitment – not in training or other human resource functions. Candidates were required to sit 'open' exams that were made available to the public (or to civil servants on lower grades). The most successful candidates would also be interviewed before selection. The security of tenure and favourable pension entitlements offered by the service, as well as the underdeveloped state of other economic sectors, ensured that the service traditionally attracted a high calibre of candidate. Over time and depending on the type of work involved, individual departments could also, with government approval, directly recruit individuals with specialist or technical skills if they believed that it was in the public interest to do so. Posts must be advertised in *Iris Oifigiúil* – the official gazette of government. In recent years the methods and organisation of recruitment to the service have changed.

As noted above, the Civil Service Regulations Act, 1956 provided for the organisational structure of the civil service. Under Section 17 of that Act, the Minister for Finance was to be responsible for setting the terms and conditions of civil servants. It also provided that every civil servant would hold office at the will and pleasure of government. In other words, civil servants could be removed only by the government. This position has changed with the Public Service Management Act, 1997, which gave Secretaries General considerable power and responsibility with respect to appointments, dismissals, performance and discipline of civil servants in their department up to the grade of Principal Officer.

Also, the Public Service Management (Recruitment and Appointments) Act, 2004 repealed the Civil Service Commissioners Act, 1956

and amended the legislation dealing with the Local Appointments
Commission. Most importantly, it altered the manner in which civil
servants are recruited by creating two new bodies:

- the Public Appointments Service
- the Commission for Public Service Appointments.

The Public Appointments Service replaces the Civil Service
Commission and the Local Appointments Commission. It acts as
a centralised recruitment, assessment and selection body for
departments and other public service bodies. It recruits new entrants to
the civil service as normal, who will then be assigned to various
departments and agencies. The Commission for Public Service
Appointments is a regulatory body that establishes and monitors
standards for recruitment to the civil service and other parts of the
bureaucracy. It licenses public service bodies such as government
departments to recruit, according to clear codes of practice, on their
own behalf or with the assistance of private sector recruitment
agencies specifically approved by the commission. Its work is
designed to offer flexibility for public service organisations to allow
them to undertake their own recruitment and therefore have the ability
to respond to changes in their recruitment needs and in the labour
market. In recent years, psychometric testing and competency-based
selection interviewing have also emerged as part of the recruitment
process.

The members of the Commission for Public Service Appointments
are:

- the Ceann Comhairle
- the Secretary General of the Department of the Taoiseach
- the Secretary General of the public service management division of
  the Department of Finance
- the Ombudsman/Information Commissioner
- the Chairman of the Standards in Public Office Commission.

Originally, seniority was the unquestioned method of promotion
for all grades in the civil service but this was gradually replaced by the
idea of competition, both internal and open. The basic principle
governing promotion today is that it is based solely on *merit*. As part of
the public service modernisation agenda, promotion is increasingly
linked to the issue of performance evaluation.

The Top Level Appointments Committee (TLAC)

Prior to the establishment of the Top Level Appointments Committee, senior civil service appointments usually came from within the same department. A new government that came to power in December 1982 made a commitment to more open competition for top civil service jobs. In 1984, the TLAC was created as an independent body to oversee senior appointments. Its main remit was to facilitate automatic interdepartmental competition for Assistant Secretary and higher posts, and to recommend candidates to ministers and government. This enhanced the management structure of the service by creating a more meritocratic system. Today, appointments above the grade of Principal Officer cannot occur without the consent of the TLAC. The TLAC process commences when either a vacancy in a TLAC grade or a new post in such a grade is notified to the TLAC secretariat. At this stage TLAC has the discretion to decide whether posts should be filled by open competition or by a competition run among eligible officers across the civil service.

The Taoiseach appoints the members of the TLAC in consultation with the Minister for Finance. There are five or six members on the Committee:

- Secretary General, Public Service Management and Development, Department of Finance (*ex officio*)
- Secretary General to the Government, Department of the Taoiseach (*ex officio*)
- a private sector member, appointed for a three-year term
- two other Secretaries General, appointed for three-year terms
- One other Secretary General, where not already a member and where a post in his/her department is being filled. Where the post being filled is below Secretary General level, he/she is present as an observer; where his/her successor is being appointed, he/she is a full member.

The TLAC does not make recommendations in relation to the filling of the following posts:

- Secretary General to the Government and to Department of the Taoiseach
- Secretary General, Department of Finance
- Secretary General, Public Service Management and Development, Department of Finance

- Secretary General, Department of Foreign Affairs
- Secretary General to the President
- Chairman, Office of the Revenue Commissioners.

These appointments are made directly by government without going through the TLAC process.

Central and line departments

Though it is not recognised in any legal form, the Department of the Taoiseach and the Department of Finance are often referred to as the 'central' departments, reflecting both the constitutional pre-eminence of the Taoiseach and Minister for Finance and these departments' involvement in all major policy and funding decisions. The departments also play important co-ordinating roles in respect of the prioritisation of national objectives and management of EU commitments. Broadly speaking, both the Department of the Taoiseach and the Department of Finance have to balance 'controlling' and 'promoting' roles with regard to the provision of public service. This is particularly the case in the Department of Finance, which has, for example, responsibility both for controlling the public service pay-bill and for management and development functions aimed at enhancing the efficiency and effectiveness of the public service.

Naturally, other ('line') departments will exercise considerable discretion and remain responsible for the direction of policy in their respective areas. In other words, while the central departments can support and persuade, they they cannot command. If differences and disagreements emerge between departments they may need to be resolved at Cabinet level. It should be noted that there are a variety of interdepartmental groups working on a variety of issues across the public service. Examples include:

- an interdepartmental committee on development
- senior officials' group on social inclusion
- high-level group on Travellers
- interdepartmental group on drugs
- interdepartmental group on private–public partnerships (PPPs)
- tax strategy group
- interdepartmental group on the review of the economic regulatory environment.

The role of these groups in the implementation of government policy is central to contemporary government, and enhances the state's ability to achieve a 'whole of government' approach to public affairs. The work and organisation of the two central departments are considered in more detail below.

The central departments – Department of the Taoiseach

The *office* of the Taoiseach was considered in Chapter 7. This office is supported in its work by the *Department* of the Taoiseach, which has grown substantially since it was created by virtue of the 1937 Constitution, and particularly since Ireland's accession to the EU in 1973.

Like any department, the Department of the Taoiseach carries out a range of functions for which its minister, the Taoiseach, is responsible to government and Dáil Éireann. However, the Department of the Taoiseach also performs functions on behalf of the government as a whole. There are approximately 220 staff in the department, of whom 190 are civil servants and the remainder political appointees with various functions.

In the first instance, the principal role of the department is to support and advise the Taoiseach in carrying out the various duties pertaining to that office. The department also provides and houses the Secretariat to the Government – whose duties include co-ordinating meetings of Cabinet sub-committees – and supplies administrative support to the government Chief Whip. The department plays a central role in acting as a link between the President, the Taoiseach and other government departments and, when Ireland holds the EU Presidency, is involved in co-ordinating meetings of the EU Council (see Chapter 19). It arranges state functions such as commemorations, Presidential inaugurations and official state dinners, as well as providing a protocol service to the Taoiseach of the day.

The principal policy areas of concern to the department include the following.

Economic and social policy

The Economic and Social Policy Division is the largest in the Department of the Taoiseach. It provides advice to the Taoiseach on economic policy and works closely with the Department of Finance. A number of agencies assist the department in this work, as follows.

- The *National Economic and Social Council* (www.nesc.ie) was established in 1973 'to advise the government on the development of the national economy and the achievement of social justice'. It produces reports on various issues concerning economic and social policy and development, and its work has provided the basis for the Social Partnership agreements (see below) since 1987. Since 2006, the work of NESC (as well as that of two other bodies – the National Economic and Social Forum (NESF) and the National Centre for Partnership and Performance (NCPP)) feeds into a body known as the National Economic and Social Development Office (NESDO), which helps to support these organisations and co-ordinate their work.

- Although it had existed within the Department of the Taoiseach since 1949, the Statistics Act of 1993 provided for the establishment of the *Central Statistics Office* (www.cso.ie) on a statutory basis and as an independent office under the aegis of that department.
- The *National Competitiveness Council* (www.forfas.ie/ncc) was established in 1997 and is required to report to the Taoiseach on key competitiveness issues for the Irish economy together with recommendations on policy actions required to enhance Ireland's competitiveness internationally. The council's secretariat is provided by Forfás – the national policy and advisory board for enterprise, trade, science, technology and innovation.

While economic issues are important to overall national development, the relationship between such issues and social policy has become more prominent in recent years. NESC defined social policy as:

> those actions of government which deliberately or accidentally affect the distribution of resources, status, opportunities and life chances among social groups and categories of people within the country and thus help to shape the general character and equity of its social relations.

Social policy therefore covers issues such as childcare, education, drugs, poverty, health and social inclusion. The Economic and Social Policy Division is also concerned with infrastructure development and PPPs, and plays a co-ordinating role in relation to the international financial services industry in Ireland.

Social partnership
Since 1987, the Irish government has engaged in partnership agreements with groups representing workers, employers and farmers

roughly every three years. More recently, the 'community and voluntary' sector has become involved with the process and the agreements are concerned with matters of social policy and justice as well as economic issues. The partners, of which government is one, negotiate on such issues as wage rates, working hours and reforms, and many argue that these agreements have provided industrial harmony and the framework for Ireland's recent economic success. The most recent partnership agreement (agreed in 2006) is called *Towards 2016* and, unlike its predecessors, is scheduled to run for 10 years.

Information Society Policy Unit
This section of the department is concerned with such issues as the construction of telecommunications infrastructure; the increased use of and access to web-based public services by Irish citizens; and developing Ireland's role as a developer of technological innovation. Reflecting wider changes in Irish society and economic life, Cabinet business is now managed through an internal system known as e-Cabinet.

Northern Ireland
Matters relating to Northern Ireland also fall within the remit of the Department of the Taoiseach. Since the signing of the Good Friday Agreement in 1998, the principal focus has been on the implementation of the agreement and the institutions created under it. As will be discussed in Chapter 18, the agreement has three interlinking elements:

- an Assembly and Executive within Northern Ireland
- North–South institutions to deal with matters of mutual concern, including a North–South Ministerial Council
- East–West institutions such as the British-Irish Council.

European and international affairs
Ireland's continued role in the European Union has transformed the manner in which government in Ireland at all levels functions. This division of the department, along with other departments such as Foreign Affairs, oversees issues emerging at European and international level of concern to Ireland. It is also involved in co-ordinating the policy approaches of government departments and other state bodies. Its principal role is to ensure that the Taoiseach is fully briefed on key developments at European and international level, and that Ireland's interests are actively pursued.

Public service modernisation
The public service modernisation process will be considered in more detail below. Co-ordination of the process is by the *Implementation Group of Secretaries General*, chaired by the Secretary General at the Department of the Taoiseach.

The central departments – Department of Finance
The importance of the correct use of the public finances is addressed in Article 17.2 of the Constitution:

> Dáil Éireann shall not pass any vote or resolution, and no law shall be enacted, for the appropriation of revenue or other public moneys unless the purpose of the appropriation shall have been recommended to Dáil Éireann by a message from the government signed by the Taoiseach.

The article places a particular responsibility on the government in order to prevent a cavalier approach to public expenditure. To this end, the Department of Finance plays a central role in managing, administering, co-ordinating, supervising and advising on the national finances (see also Chapter 11). The 1924 Ministers and Secretaries Act explicitly stated that the Department of Finance was to be responsible for:

> the administration and business generally of the public finance of Ireland and all powers, duties and functions connected with the same, including in particular, the collection and expenditure of the revenues of Ireland from whatever source arising.

However, the responsibilities and functional areas under the remit of the Department of Finance have expanded since then. The Economic Planning and Development (Transfer of Departmental Administration and Ministerial Functions) Order, 1980 gave additional functions to the Department of Finance:

* promoting and co-ordinating economic and social planning
* identifying development policies
* reviewing the methods adopted by departments of state to implement such policies
* advising the government on economic and social planning matters.

Also, the Department of Finance is the only department to receive particular recognition in the Constitution. This is not surprising given that the business of governing is expensive. Modern states collect and spend huge sums of money and it is logical that this activity be co-ordinated to maximise its effectiveness. The department acts as economic adviser to the government through the Minister for Finance, and regulates the financial and administrative system as a whole. This includes responsibility for public expenditure, taxation, the Budget, economic policy and the management of the public service. Today, with the exception of commercial rates, which are decided on by local authorities, the department retains control over all forms of national taxation, including income tax, corporation tax, value added tax, capital gains tax, stamp duties, capital acquisitions taxes (gift tax and inheritance tax), residential property tax, certain Customs and Excise duties, and motor vehicle registration tax. There are six divisions in the Department of Finance, as follows.

1. *Sectoral Policy Division (SPD)*. This is concerned with the activities of all departments and agencies. Its role is to ensure that expenditure by public service bodies is in keeping with overall government policy, and to evaluate the estimates put forward by these bodies each year before reporting to the Minister for Finance. This division also assists the Committee of Public Accounts.

2. *Taxation and Financial Services Division (TFSD)*. This division is concerned with how money is raised by the state through taxes and borrowing and also from EU transfers. In this role it regulates borrowing by other public organisations and works closely with the Central Bank and international organisations such as the European Investment Bank and International Monetary Fund.

3. *Budget, Economic and Pensions Division (BEPD)*. The work of this division centres on the development and performance of the Irish economy, including taxation policy. In this role, it prepares forecasts and briefs international bodies on the Irish economy. It also prepares the annual financial statements for the minister and the finance bill that enacts the measures outlined in the Budget.

4. *Personnel and Remuneration Division (PRD)*. This division considers the pay and conditions of the public sector, as well as issues related to human resources management such as recruitment and promotion in the sector.

5. *Organisation, Management and Training Division (OMTD)*. The role of this division is to take overall responsibility for the management and development of the civil service, including the identification of the most appropriate organisational structures and

training to maximise efficiency. It is aided by the Civil Service Centre for Management and Organisation Development (CMOD) and the Corporate Services Division (CSD).

6. *Corporate Services.* As in other departments, the CSD is involved with issues of internal staffing, accommodation, and co-ordination of strategic management in the department.

The Department of Finance also has several agencies in its remit, including the following.

- The *National Treasury Management Agency* (NTMA), which was established in 1990 to raise the funds necessary to finance the government's borrowing requirement, and to advise the department and minister on the management of the national debt. The NTMA also manages the National Pensions Reserve Fund and other funds such as the Dormant Accounts Fund. In addition, the provision of financial advice as well as guarantees for all major public investment projects is carried out by the National Development Finance Agency operating through the NTMA.

- The *Office of the Revenue Commissioners* was established in 1923. Its principal duty is to collect taxes, which go towards funding the exchequer, and it employs approximately 7,000 staff in over 100 offices nationwide.

- The *Office of the Appeal Commissioners* hears appeals by taxpayers against the decisions of the Revenue Commissioners concerning taxes and duties controlled by the state.

Public service reform

Governments frequently propose administrative reform, but the details of such reforms tend not to carry much public interest. The Irish public service is currently undergoing the most sustained period of reform in its history. Before considering this in detail, a number of previous reform attempts should be mentioned.

Report of the Commission on the Civil Service (The Brennan Commission)

A decade after the transfer of administrative functions from British to Irish Free State control, a commission was established (under the chairmanship of former Secretary General at the Department of Finance Joseph Brennan) to inquire into and report on the recruitment and organisation of the civil service with special reference to the arrangements for ensuring efficiency in working.[17]

It produced an interim report in 1934 and a final report in 1935. It noted how the Ministers and Secretaries Act of 1924 had played an important role in allowing the new state to subsume the functions of many existing boards and commissions into government departments, and that many calls for greater co-ordination of the civil service came from within that service rather than outside it. The commission considered such issues as control and regulation of the civil service but its final report found the system to be satisfactory overall, and consequently did not lead to any substantial reordering.

The Devlin Report, 1969

While the civil service capably performed many modest functions without difficulty for several decades after independence, from the 1950s onwards the need for a more creative and policy-oriented service became apparent. It was also recognised that greater efforts at co-ordination were required. The impetus for change led to the Public Services Organisation Review Group being established in 1966, under the chairmanship of Liam Devlin. Its mandate was as follows:

> Having regard to the growing responsibilities of Government, to examine and report on the organisation of the Departments of State ... including the appropriate distribution of functions as between both Departments themselves and Departments and other bodies.[18]

Its final report was a weighty volume that surveyed, critiqued and proposed widespread reform of the service, based on two underlying principles:

1. a greater emphasis on policy-making
2. the need for greater integration and co-ordination in the public service.

---

[17] Fanning, R. (1978) *The Irish Department of Finance 1922–58*. Dublin: Institute of Public Administration, p. 241.

[18] Institute of Public Administration (1970) *The Devlin Report: A Summary*. Dublin: IPA, p. 3.

The most radical reform recommended by the Report was the division of each government department along policy development and execution lines. The policy-making core of the department would be called the *Aireacht* and it would have responsibility for overall planning, direction and control, subject to the minister and government's approval. The rest of the department would be concerned with policy implementation, and would comprise a number of 'satellite' bodies (or 'executive agencies'). The report also called for the integration of general service, departmental and technical/professional staff, and the establishment of a new Public Service Department. While this last recommendation did occur, for a variety of reasons the main proposals were not acted upon.

Serving the Country Better, 1985

In 1983, a new government committed to public service reform established the National Planning Board to create a new national economic plan. This plan was called *Building on Reality* and made a commitment to widespread institutional reform in the public sector. It resulted in the White Paper *Serving the Country Better*, which was published in 1985. The paper was aimed at improving the efficiency and effectiveness of the civil service and envisaged the introduction of a management system based on corporate planning and personal responsibility for results, costs and service. However, the enabling legislation was stalled by the acute economic crisis of the period, and the paper's proposals never entered the Dáil or Seanad for debate.

Public sector reforms following the White Paper were largely incremental and uncoordinated. Also, an emphasis on controlling expenditure and personnel numbers (including an embargo on recruitment in 1987) dominated government thinking with respect to the civil service. Nonetheless, some important changes occurred. In 1987 the Department of Public Service was merged with the Department of Finance. In 1989–1990 over a thousand civil servants were decentralised to regional centres. An Efficiency Audit Group was established in 1989 to survey the practices of government departments and to report recommendations for improving efficiency and reducing costs. The issue of performance-related pay was introduced in 1990 for the Assistant Secretary grade. In 1991, administrative budgets were introduced in most civil service departments with the aim of increasing the effectiveness of government expenditure by augmenting the flexibility and accountability of line managers.

From public administration to public management:
The introduction of the Strategic Management Initiative

Impetus for more systemic reform gathered pace during the early 1990s as the Irish economy began to develop rapidly and international ideas concerning public service performance gained popularity. The EU also played a role in encouraging change. This culminated in the launch of a new programme for reform in 1994, known as the Strategic Management Initiative (SMI).

As its name suggests, the SMI involved the import of many private sector ideas concerning management and strategic planning, and called for a strategic approach by civil servants based on the need for better planning and management. The public service, it was argued, could be better delivered if administrators were more like 'managers', with agreed goals and related output targets. Furthermore, the programme envisaged reform not just in the civil service but across the public service, including the local government and health sectors.

In essence, SMI was designed to address three key areas:

* enhanced contribution of the public service to national development
* provision of top-quality services in a timely and efficient manner
* effective use of available resources.

The SMI was launched by Taoiseach Albert Reynolds in 1994, marking the enthusiastic political endorsement of a movement already under way. It set out a schedule of change, starting with the preparation of plans for the various parts of the public service. Government departments published their first statements of strategy in 1995. In order to reflect its public sector focus, after a few years the name Strategic Management Initiative was replaced by *Public Service Modernisation Programme*. Responsibility for its development remains with the Department of the Taoiseach.

Another important development in the modernisation process was the creation of a Co-ordinating Group of Secretaries General drawn from nine departments, with a mandate to oversee and direct the initiative and report to government on its progress. This group produced the report that has informed the civil service reform process – *Delivering Better Government: A Programme of Change for the Irish Civil Service* (DBG).[19]

---

[19] A similar programme was launched for local government around the same period, titled *Better Local Government* (see Chapter 12)

Delivering Better Government placed a strong emphasis on the need for extensive consultation at all levels of the public service. Several major initiatives, which are ongoing, were instigated in the years after it was launched, including:

- the *Quality Customer Service Initiative* (1997)
- a *Review of Public Expenditure* (1997)
- *Performance Management and Development Systems* (2000).

An *Implementation Group of Secretaries General* was also established in 1997 to help with the 'roll-out' of DBG, and is chaired by the Secretary to the Department of the Taoiseach. The Department of Finance has particular responsibility with regard to human resource and financial management reform initiatives, as well as progressing the necessary legislative change (e.g. the Public Service Management (Recruitment and Appointments) Act, 2004).

DBG identified six areas or 'levers of change' that the civil service needed to address:

1. quality customer services
2. regulatory reform
3. openness and transparency
4. human resource management
5. financial management
6. information technology.

1. Quality customer services
A core part of the SMI agenda is the recognition of citizens as 'customers' in the delivery service. In 1997, a *Quality Customer Service Initiative* was launched which obliged public organisations to issue statements of service standards. All departments must also now produce 'Customer Action Plans' that detail how they will improve service delivery, and mechanisms for customer complaints and redress have been put in place. A Civil Service Quality Assurance Group was also established and a biannual awards scheme for public service excellence initiated. In 2003, customer charters were introduced in all central government departments and offices. These were reviewed and a report guiding their further enhancement was produced in 2007. Subsequently, a Task Force on Customer Service was established, chaired by the Secretary General at the Department of Justice, Equality and Law Reform, to advance the proposals made in the report and to

develop customer services more generally. Important strides have also been made in relation to the provision of public services online (see below). A set of Principles for Quality Customer Service was introduced and expanded upon in 2000.[20]

2. Regulatory reform

Regulatory reform has been a key feature of the SMI process. As noted earlier, the role of the state is not only to provide services but also to regulate them. In 1999 the government produced a report entitled *Reducing Red Tape: An Action Programme of Regulatory Reform in Ireland.* Among other things, the report sought to improve the quality of regulations, eliminate inefficient ones, and lower the cost of regulatory compliance. As well as being an integral part of the modernisation agenda, pressure for regulatory reform emanated from the EU and the OECD (see Chapter 20), the latter of which produced another report on Irish regulatory reform in 2001. It defined regulation as 'the diverse set of instruments by which governments set requirements on enterprises and citizens'.[21] Developing this, the report identified three forms of regulation, as follows.

* *Economic:* Regulatory reforms in the economy are designed to reduce barriers to competition, and to provide mechanisms for adequate oversight of sectors of the economy. This latter aspect has involved the creation of a number of regulators for specific sectors of the economy, e.g. a telecommunications regulator (ComReg), the Commission for Energy Regulation and the Commission for Aviation Regulation.
* *Social:* Regulatory reforms in the social realm are aimed at ensuring that public interests such as health and education are not over-regulated so that they may be provided effectively.
* *Administrative:* Regulatory reform in this field aims to reduce the form-filling and bureaucratic requirements on businesses and individuals that seek to access services or perform certain functions such as marketplace trading.

---

[20] These principles cover quality service standards, equality/diversity, physical access, information, timeliness and courtesy, complaints, appeals, consultation and evaluation, choice, official languages equality, better co-ordination and internal customer.
[21] OECD (2001) *Regulatory Reform in Ireland.* Paris: OECD, p. 17.

Since the OECD report was launched there have been a number of further developments in the area of regulation, including a government White Paper entitled *Regulating Better* in 2004 which set out principles for better regulation.[22] Also, a process known as regulatory impact analysis (RIA) has been introduced which requires departments to identify and, where possible, quantify the impact of new regulations on a range of areas. The rationale of RIA is that it will allow for better and more informed decision-making. Other developments include reform of statute law, which involved the repeal of hundreds of outdated laws as well as the consolidation or restatement of more recent legislation.

3. Openness and transparency

The most important step taken with respect to this element of the modernisation programme is the Freedom of Information Act, 1997. The Act came into effect on 21 April 1998 and introduced the legal right for people:

- to access official records held by government departments and other listed public bodies
- to have personal information held on them corrected or updated where such information is incomplete, incorrect or misleading
- to be given reasons for decisions taken by public bodies that affect them.

Subsequent amendments to the legislation curtailed some aspects of the original Act but almost all public bodies (exceptions include the Gardaí and hospitals) are required to have mechanisms in place for public access to documents as appropriate. The Act also provided for the creation of the Office of the Information Commissioner, a position that has been combined with that of the Ombudsman (see below). The role of the Information Commissioner includes reviewing decisions made by public bodies in relation to FOI requests, keeping the operation of the Act under review with a view to ensuring maximum compliance, encouraging a culture of transparency within the public service, and producing reports on the operation of the Act.

---

[22] These are necessity, effectiveness, proportionality, transparency, accountability and consistency.

Records that are exempt from the Act include:

- Cabinet documents, related briefings and records of certain committees (for a period of 10 years)
- documents relating to key areas of government activity
- records relating to law enforcement, security, international relations and Northern Ireland
- records whose release might damage the economic interests of the state
- records subject to legal professional privilege, and certain matters relating to the courts, the Oireachtas and tribunals
- records relating to research and natural resources.

4. Human resource management

The modernisation project acknowledges that for medium- and long-term goals to be met, staff training and upskilling is necessary, as well as more flexible working arrangements. Performance Management and Development Systems (PMDS) were introduced in 2000; they involve all civil servants meeting with their line managers to discuss targets and agree work practices that will contribute to achieving the departmental strategic objectives and business plans. Other human resource management developments included the devolution of staff recruitment from a centralised system to one based around organisations such as individual government departments. This has also been rolled out to other parts of the public administration, such as the local government system. Related to the issue of performance, two 'benchmarking' studies (published in 2002 and 2007) have compared public sector remuneration with that of equivalent roles in the private sector. New management and human resources practices were put on a legislative footing with the 2005 Civil Service Regulation Act.

5. Financial management

Prior to SMI, the introduction of administrative budgets for line departments in 1991 was probably one of the most important reform measures to date. Budgets were set for three years by agreement between the Department of Finance and each line department, and covered all aspects of spending, including training, travel and subsistence, and salaries and wages. The idea was to improve administrative efficiency and the effectiveness of spending programmes by the delegation of authority for decision-making from Finance to departmental management within each department. Also, five-year capital programmes have been introduced in all relevant departments (except Transport, where multi-annual programmes are for 10 years). To assist in the roll-out of capital programmes, the Department of Finance has developed guidelines for their appraisal and management.

The DBG programme envisaged delegating increased levels of financial autonomy to departments, as well as better systems of audit. Also, methods for assessing value for money have been introduced, and are complemented by the work of the Comptroller and Auditor General (see Chapter 11). In 1997, an Expenditure Review Initiative (ERI) was launched which was later followed by a new Management Information Framework (MIF) to provide stronger links between resource inputs and performance. The purpose of the ERI is to analyse public expenditure and to provide more informed decision-making about government programmes. Also, MIF Steering Groups were established in each department. Two reports have been produced, in 2001 and 2004, and a Central Expenditure Evaluation Unit was established within the Department of Finance in 2006. The main functions of this unit include evaluation of the National Development Plan and compliance with value-for-money frameworks for capital expenditure. Also, Budget 2006 was used to initiate a new departure whereby information on outputs and the achievement of objectives would be published by departments alongside financial information as and from 2007.

6. Information technology
As with the private sector, public services have increasingly resorted to electronic means of communication and information storage. As part of an ongoing 'eGovernment' programme, increasing amounts of information concerning the civil service are now available online, and all departments have intranet facilities for internal communications. Also, in 2004 the 'e-Cabinet' initiative was launched, which electronically manages Cabinet documentation. The initiative was designed to reduce the manual process of preparing, refining and circulating documentation for Cabinet. Greater online provision of public services has also been a feature of this element of the modernisation agenda, though progress has been slower than anticipated. For example, an initiative known as *Reach* (www.reachservices.ie) provides members of the public with a virtual 'one-stop shop' for information on all public services and entitlements. The initiative involved the establishment of an agency in 2001 (also known as Reach) to lead and manage the programme, which involved extensive co-operation

between the Departments of the Taoiseach, Finance and Social and Family Affairs as well as the Revenue Commissioners. In May 2008, the newly elected Taoiseach Brian Cowen announced that responsibility for the eGovernment programme was to be transferred from his Department to the Department of Finance.

Public Service Management Act, 1997

The changes in the Irish civil service as a result of the modernisation programme demanded that the legislation underpinning the civil service be reappraised. Following a review of the Ministers and Secretaries Acts, 1924 to 1991, designed to bring about a greater focus on service delivery, performance and the achievement of results, the Public Service Management Act, 1997 became law. This was consistent with the SMI themes of devolving authority and accountability in the public service.

The Act gives a legal basis for the new management structures to enhance the management, effectiveness and transparency of operations of departments and offices of the public service. It provides for increased accountability of civil servants while preserving the discretion of the government in relation to their responsibility to Dáil Éireann, and for the administration of departments and offices, the appointment of special advisers, assignment of cross-departmental functions and the corporate status of certain public offices. It also provides a legal basis for the requirement on each department to prepare a strategy statement (see above) every three years, or within six months of the appointment of a new minister.

In relation to the policy administration divide, the Act specifies that the responsibility for policy objectives and agreeing necessary results lies with ministers, while Secretaries General advise ministers and ensure their department produces the necessary results. Although based on the principle of ministerial accountability to the Dail, the 1997 Act provides that the traditional role of senior civil servants as policy advisers be complemented by an enhanced role as 'managers' of the service. There is now more emphasis on delegation of functions, policy appraisal, strategic and performance management, and ensuring that appropriate accountability procedures are in place. The managerial role of Secretaries General is much more explicit as a result of the Act.

In summary, the principles of the legislation are as follows.

- The Secretary General of a department has the authority, responsibility, and accountability for managing the department, implementing government policies, and delivering outputs as determined by the minister.

- She or he is responsible for managing 'all matters pertaining to appointments, performance, discipline and dismissals of staff below the grade of principal officer'.
- She or he is responsible for assigning responsibility to grades 'down the line' for the provision of policy advice, the achievement of specified outputs, the delivery of quality service in a particular area, and the proper management of human and financial resources.
- In short, the Secretary General is responsible for the management of his or her department. He or she will advise the minister on policy and prepare strategy statements for authorisation by the minister that show what outputs are required to meet the outcomes specified in the policy.

Codes of Conduct
In the midst of the multiple reform agendas that constitute the public service modernisation agenda, the public service is expected to remain true to its core values, including integrity, fairness, impartiality and honesty. To support this, Codes of Conduct have emerged for various parts of the service. Codes of Conduct are a form of voluntary oversight that establishes the parameters of the work of those in a given profession. Indeed, one of the principal features of Codes of Conduct is that they are normally not legally binding, but are instead enforced by those within the profession in question.

In September 2004, the Minister for Finance launched the new Civil Service Code of Standards and Behaviour. This was a requirement under the Standards in Public Office Act, 2001. Apart from identifying the values and expected behaviour of civil servants, the code established rules pertaining to potential conflicts of interest. It followed the production of similar codes for ministers, TDs and Senators, and local government officials and elected members.

The Civil Service Code states that:

The mission of the Civil Service is the achievement of an excellent service for Government and the other institutions of State as well as for the public as citizens and users of public services, based on principles of integrity, impartiality, effectiveness, equity and accountability.

Evaluating and developing the modernisation programme
The Department of the Taoiseach commissioned a consultancy (PA Consulting) to assess progress with respect to reform of the civil service in July 2001. The terms of reference for the assignment called for a quantitative and a qualitative evaluation of progress achieved. The central question addressed by the consultants was – 'What impact did the application of SMI/DBG have across the civil service, and has the service received by the customer improved as a consequence?' The report found that 'the civil service in 2002 is a more effective organisation than it was a decade earlier', but also noted that the programme was far from complete. In particular, it saw the deeper engagement of politicians in the process as critical to its development. A special report by the Comptroller and Auditor General in 2007 suggested that 'while [reform] initiatives have been co-ordinated, the achievement of results has been incremental and institution specific',[23] and that:

> While progress has been made on modernisation in the areas of strategic planning, HRM and programme evaluation, there is a need to review the extent to which the modernisation programme is impacting on value in the form of improved services or more efficient processes.

It also proposed that the next phase of the modernisation agenda required a 'stronger and more measurable set of targets for improvement' as well as 'a more coherent and integrated vision supported by specified modernisation objectives'.

A major programme of civil service relocation or 'decentralisation' was announced in 2003 with the aim of moving over 10,000 civil servants out of Dublin to locations throughout the state. A Decentralisation Implementation Group was established to oversee progress. While initial plans were for the process to be completed by the end of 2007, at the time of writing this target had not been met and the overall development of the programme has been slow.

The most recent plans to advance the reform agenda were announced in 2006 by the Taoiseach, and included:

---

[23] Office of the Comptroller and Auditor General (2007) *Improving Performance: Public Service Case Studies.* Dublin, pp. 23–25.

- benchmarking the work of departments with counterparts elsewhere
- the development of new methods for reporting to parliament on administrative performance
- the development of leadership skills in the public service.

Also, in 2006 the OECD was invited to initiate a system-wide review of the Irish public service and to benchmark it with comparable countries across the OECD. The final report on this work – *Towards an Integrated Public Service* (available at www.bettergov.ie) – was a substantial volume published in April 2008. As its name suggests, instead of any significant institutional reform, the study called for greater connectivity and linkages across the public service, and particularly between the local government, civil service and state agency sectors. Other principal recommendations included:

- the enhancement of performance management and use of performance information in decision-making
- improved roll-out of eGovernment initiatives and the use of ICT to deliver integrated services
- greater use of collaborative networks within and across public service organisations
- greater movement of personnel between the various parts of the public service, including the establishment of a 'Senior Public Service' to encourage mobility at the senior management levels.

At the time of writing, the government had appointed a nine-member task force to develop an action plan for future public service reform in light of the OECD report.

The Office of the Ombudsman
As noted above, civil servants have traditionally been hierarchically accountable for their work to their senior managers, with ministers ultimately collectively responsible to the Dáil for the work of the service. However, as Chapter 6 has detailed, since 1997 civil servants may also be asked to appear before Oireachtas committees to answer questions concerning the implementation of policies without expressing opinions on their merits or objectives. Another important mechanism for ensuring good administration and investigating maladministration is the Office of the Ombudsman.

The word 'Ombudsman' is Swedish in origin and means a representative or agent of the people. The King of Sweden appointed the first Office of the Parliamentary Ombudsman in 1809 to investigate complaints against his ministers. Since then, other states have established equivalent offices; the past 30 years has seen an explosion in the number of Ombudsman offices in Europe – not only for public administration, but also for sectoral issues (such as the insurance industry) or for certain social groups (such as children). The role of an Ombudsman in terms of administration is to promote good administrative behaviour not only strictly with regard to the law but also with regard to what is considered fair and reasonable.

The Ombudsman Act of 1980 provided for the office in Ireland, but the first office-holder was not appointed until 1984. He or she is appointed by the President on the nomination of the Dáil and Seanad. The Ombudsman (who, since 1997, is also the Information Commissioner) examines complaints from members of the public who feel that they have been the victim of maladministration. He or she has power to access documents and files in most, but not all, aspects of the public administration, and can request persons who have information to attend before him/her. Areas outside the Ombudsman's remit include the police (a separate Garda Ombudsman Commission was established in 2007), third-level education institutions, prison administration and hospitals. The office received over 2,000 valid complaints in 2006. Decisions of the Ombudsman are not legally binding but carry significant moral and persuasive influence, and public bodies tend to accede to his or her findings and recommendations on matters. The Ombudman's annual reports (and any special reports) are presented to the Houses of the Oireachtas.

9

State agencies

The boundaries between public and private in Ireland have never been clearly demarcated and continue to be blurred by developments described in this volume. The legacy of a variety of organisations involved to various degrees in public services at the time of Independence, as well as the establishment of many others since then under a multitude of legal frameworks, makes the limits of the state difficult to identify. So too does the involvement of an assortment of non-governmental organisations (including religious orders) in public service delivery. While a detailed examination of the various forms, methods, tasks and legal provisions for public service is not possible here, in this chapter I do wish to consider the role of what have come to be known as 'state agencies'.

As demands on the public service have increased, so too have the requirements for specialist skills, political independence, cross-departmental collaboration and new modes of service delivery in a variety of policy areas. In response to these (and other) dynamics, many functions of the departmental civil service have been devolved to stand-alone organisations or 'agencies' that exist outside of the traditional structures of government departments. While ministers remain ultimately responsible to parliament for most of these bodies, their level of day-to-day involvement and management of their affairs is not the same as for their department generally.

A variety of terms are used in Ireland and elsewhere to describe these bodies, including 'quango' (quasi-autonomous non-governmental organisation), 'semi-state body' and 'state-sponsored body'. Internationally, while considerable differences exist according to administrative cultures and legal and political systems, the term 'agency' has come into common currency and the process of establishing agencies – 'agencification' – is recognised as a phenomenon of modern public administration. In this chapter, the focus is on non-trading agencies, which are to be distinguished from those public sector organisations that are also (largely) independent of government departments but that act in a commercial manner or perform commercial functions. Such commercial agencies or 'state enterprises' are considered in the next chapter. Also, the agencies discussed here include specialist units established within departments under the direct control of a minister (and which may or may not have a legal personality of their own) – these are often referred to as executive or advisory agencies/offices. Examples include the Irish Naturalisation and Immigration Service (INIS) or the Reception Integration Agency (RIA) within the Department of Justice, Equality and Law Reform (see Figure 9.1). By contrast, this department also has a number of statutory agencies under its remit, including the Property Registration Authority and the Equality Authority, each with its own board.

Figure 9.1. *Internal (executive) and external (statutory) agencies*

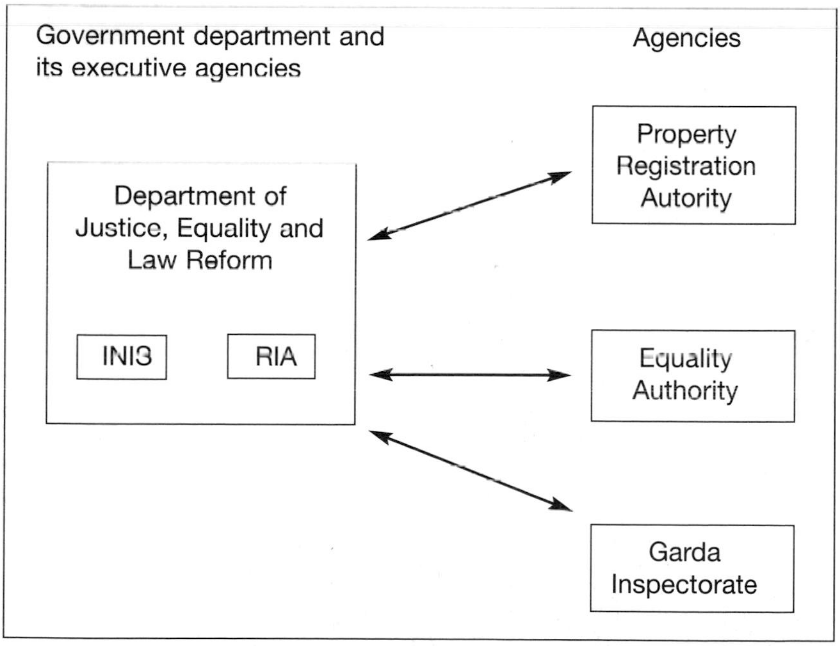

While the creation of public service bodies outside of departmental structures is not necessarily a new phenomenon – agencies such as the Irish Film Censor's Office having been established within a year of Independence – what is significant is the number of such bodies currently in existence and the speed with which many of them have been created since the early 1990s. At national level (Chapter 12 will consider those agencies at sub-national level) there are now approximately 200 agencies involved in a wide range of public service activity, each with its own structure, legal status and accountability relationship to its 'parent' department and minister.

Some examples of recently established agencies are given in Table 9.1.

Table 9.1. *Some recently established agencies*

New agency	Parent or funding department	Year of establish-ment	Reason for establishment
Garda Ombudsman Commission	Justice, Equality and Law Reform	2007	Need for independent oversight of policing matters
Road Safety Authority	Transport	2006	Combines duties of former National Safety Council with new road safety functions
Irish Auditing and Accounting Supervisory Authority	Enterprise, Trade and Employment	2005	Need for independent oversight of accountancy profession
Health Services Executive	Health	2005	Rationalisation of health services management and service delivery
Public Appointments Service	Finance	2004	Dissolution and replacement of the Office of the Civil Service and Local Appointments Commissioners
Commission for Taxi Regulation	Transport	2004	Need for independent regulation of taxi industry

Unlike many other European states, where the development of·the administrative system is informed by a large body of administrative law and agencies can be categorised accordingly, in Ireland agencies have emerged through a variety of means and legislative instruments, and categorisation is difficult. The majority of recently established agencies are created by an Act of the Oireachtas that establishes their remit, funding arrangements, level of independence and accountability arrangements. Such agencies are often referred to as *statutory corporations* or *statutory bodies*, i.e. they have a legal personality of their own which is separate from that of the department that oversees their work. In such a situation, the agency derives its powers and authority directly from its founding legislation, which may also detail its relationship with the minister and how the board of the agency is to be composed. Some agencies, which are also corporate bodies, are created by secondary legislation (e.g. regulations or ministerial orders) and may be guided by articles of association rather than by legislation.

A small number of agencies are registered as companies with the Companies Registration Office (itself an agency) and must adhere to the rules of the various pieces of legislation governing companies (the Companies Acts). The main company form used by public agencies, as well as voluntary sector agencies, is the company limited by guarantee. This is a company with no share capital. Such companies are legally independent of ministers but, because of their dependence on the state for substantial parts of their finance, may be considered as part of the public service. Where appropriate such companies may apply for charitable status, which gives certain tax advantages to non-profit organisations.

In terms of function, while the work of agencies may be categorised in various ways, a study published in 2005 found that the national-level agencies considered their principal duties as being provision of advice, implementation of policy, regulation and provision of information.[24] Most non-commercial agencies rely on a grant-in-aid from their parent department to fund their work, though some may also charge fees for services or the provision of licences. Many regulatory agencies also charge a levy on the organisations (public and/or private) whose activities they regulate. In line with the public service modernisation agenda in the civil service, many agencies must produce strategic plans which chart a course of action for three to five years ahead; customer charters for agencies are also common. In terms of accountability, most

---

[24] McGauran, A.-M., Verhoest, K. and Humphreys, P. (2005) *The Corporate Governance of Agencies in Ireland: Non-Commercial National Agencies.* Committee for Public Management Research Report No. 6. Dublin: Institute of Public Administration, p. 50.

agencies produce annual reports (including annual financial statements) to their parent departments reporting on progress, though some (such as the various Ombudsman offices or the Standards in Public Office Commission) present reports directly to the Houses of the Oireachtas. Most agencies are also subject to the requirements of the Freedom of Information Act, audit by the Comptroller and Auditor General and other public accountability requirements.

As noted above, while some agencies are staffed by civil servants, others use their own grading structure – in many cases this will parallel the terms and conditions for grades in the civil service, and staff can participate in civil service pension schemes. Other agencies, by virtue of their specialist work and need for highly trained staff, operate distinctive grading and remuneration scales. State agency staff may also be employed on contracts that are different to those of departmental civil servants (who are permanently employed directly by the government) and staff cannot move between agencies as occurs with departmental civil servants.

Boards

Normally, the work of a state agency is overseen by a committee usually known as a 'board'.[25] Board members play a very important role in the governance of agencies, and it is to the board that the chief executive and his team must provide an account of their activities. In 2001 the Department of Finance published a *Code of Practice for the Governance of State Bodies* to provide guidance for board members in carrying out their duties. A follow-up guide for board members of commercial and non-commercial state bodies identified the key roles of the board as:

• providing leadership and strategic direction
• defining control mechanisms to safeguard public resources
• supervising the overall management of the body's activities
• reporting on stewardship and performance.[26]

---

[25] Some agencies have 'commissions' or 'authorities' instead of boards.
[26] Institute of Public Administration and Chartered Institute of Public Finance and Accountancy (2002) *On Board: A Guide for Board Members of State Bodies in Ireland*. Dublin: Institute of Public Administration.

In general, the board and chairperson of an agency will report to the minister, who is obliged to attend the Dáil or one of its committees to answer questions on the conduct, performance or even problems facing the agencies reporting to his or her department. Senior executives will also communicate with civil servants from the parent department. The department therefore provides the day-to-day links between the agency and the minister.

Just as agencies vary, so too does the composition of boards. Normally, a minister will have the power to appoint some if not all of the board members to committees under his or her aegis. However, he or she may be obliged to appoint individuals from particular interest groups or affected parties. For example, the legislation for the board of the Private Security Authority, established in 2004, specified the conditions given in Table 9.2.

As new agencies continue to be established, it is important to recognise how they have changed the landscape of Irish public administration and demonstrated the ability of that administration to respond to new methods of service delivery. However, the evidence that they are delivering on the promise of better and more efficient service delivery is not conclusive, and the successful performance of an agency depends on more that its independence. Also, historical and international experience has demonstrated that processes of agencification are often followed by periods of recentralisation or reintegration of functions within departments. Indeed, there has been some rationalisation of agencies in Ireland in recent years, most notably in the health sector (see Chapter 13) with the establishment of the Health Services Executive, which assumed the functions of several existing agencies. Ensuring policy coherence between agencies and their departments, as well as between agencies, will therefore continue to be a challenge for both government and the civil service.

Table 9.2. *Private Security Authority conditions*

Section 7

(1) (*a*) The Authority shall consist of not more than 11 members.

   (*b*) Notwithstanding *paragraph (a)*, until the first appointment to the Authority of a person elected by its staff in accordance with *subsection (2)(g)*, the Authority shall consist of not more than 10 members.

   (*c*) The members of the Authority shall be appointed by the Minister, who shall designate one of them as its chairperson.

Table 9.2. *Private Security Authority conditions (contd.)*

---

(2) The members of the Authority shall include –
  (*a*) at least one person who is a practising barrister, or practising solicitor, of not less than 5 years' standing,
  (*b*) 2 persons each of whom the Minister considers to be representative of private security employers,
  (*c*) 2 persons each of whom the Minister considers to be representative of employees of such employers,
  (*d*) the Commissioner of the Garda Síochána or such other member of the Garda Síochána not below the rank of Assistant Commissioner as the Commissioner may nominate in that behalf,
  (*e*) an officer of the Minister,
  (*f*) a representative of any other Minister of the Government who, in the opinion of the Minister, is directly concerned with or responsible for activities relevant to the functions of the Authority, and
  (*g*) one member of the staff of the Authority elected by secret ballot of the staff of the Authority in such manner –
    (i) if notice of the holding of the first such election is given before the day on which the Authority is established, as the Minister directs in writing, or
    (ii) in any other case, as the Authority, with the agreement of the Minister, may determine.

10

State enterprises

In the previous chapter, bodies established outside traditional government department structures to perform certain public functions were discussed. Such state agencies are normally principally funded by the state and are not extensively involved in the trading of goods and services. However, the Irish state also owns several organisations that are involved in commercial or trading activity in sectors as diverse as seaweed harvesting, greyhound racing and health insurance. These bodies employ thousands of people and at a minimum are expected to fund their own activities. Some of them are as old as the state itself and are variously (and confusingly) referred to as state-sponsored bodies, commercial semi-state companies and, more recently, state-owned enterprises. They are referred to here simply as state enterprises (see Table 10.1).

Some of the largest and best known companies in Ireland today, such as the Electricity Supply Board (ESB) and Aer Lingus, were established as state enterprises in the early years of Independence as the new state sought to develop its infrastructure in the absence of any private sector interest in filling major gaps in the economy necessary for such development. The state also wished to exploit some of its natural resources for the benefit of the country as a whole. Since then, the Irish state has at various times sought to involve itself in other commercial activities for a variety of reasons, including employment, although many state enterprises have ceased trading or been sold. For example, during the Second World War Tea Importers Ltd and Grain Importers Ltd were established during a period of rationing of foodstuffs.

In terms of legal status, there are two principal categories of state enterprise – those established as statutory corporations by a piece of legislation that details their role, relationship to government and other such details, and those established as companies and which are incorporated under the Companies Acts.[27] The latter may be either

---

[27] The term 'Teo.' or 'Teoranta' is often used to denote limited companies.

Table 10.1. *State enterprises*

Name	Year established	Form of establishment	Function	Current status
Electricity Supply Board	1927	Statutory corporation	Provision of energy	100% state-owned
Aer Lingus	1936	Private company	Commercial air transport	25% state-owned, 75% privately owned
Bord na Móna	1946	Statutory corporation	Provision of energy	100% state-owned
Agricultural Credit Corporation (later ACC Bank)	1927	Public company	Provision of agricultural credit	Sold in 2002
Córas Iompair Éireann	1950	Statutory corporation	Public rail and road transport	100% state-owned
Voluntary Health Insurance	1957	Statutory corporation	Provision of health insurance schemes	100% state-owned
Bord Fáilte	1939	Statutory corporation	Tourism Promotion	Replaced by Fáilte Ireland in 2003
Arramara Teo.	1947	Private company	Seaweed products	82% state-owned, 18% privately owned
Port companies (e.g. Dundalk, New Ross)	1996	Private companies	Provision of port facilities	100% state-owned

public (whereby they are listed on the stock exchange, often with the letters 'plc' after them) or private (unlisted). For many enterprises under this second category, legislation has also been passed by the Oireachtas providing for their establishment, but the actual details of the establishment is conducted in line with the Companies Acts.

For many decades, state enterprises were regarded as integral parts of Irish economic life and their products and services were associated with national identity and development. While state supports and subsidies for large (and small) enterprises are today regarded as uneconomic and uncompetitive, for the first few decades of the state's existence they were regarded as essential for developing enterprise and providing employment. In recent decades governments have decided to sell or 'privatise' some of these enterprises as it was no longer felt necessary for the state to provide the service or product in question, and the Irish economy has grown to a point where it can sustain many large private enterprises offering similar services. Examples of full and partial privatisations include Irish Sugar Ltd (1991), Eircom (1999), ACC Bank (2002) and Aer Lingus (2006 — though the government retained a minority shareholding).

Most commercial enterprises derive the bulk of their revenue from trading and commercial activities, as they produce goods and services that are sold directly to the public. Several (e.g. VHI and ESB) are legally required to break even each year. A number of others, although commercial and selling services, have some social obligations; for example, the Coras Iompair Éireann (CIÉ) companies must operate public transport routes that may be uneconomical but provide an important public service. The performance of such services is often subsidised by the state. Nonetheless there is increasing emphasis on enterprises being commercially viable and self-funding. Some commercial agencies raise a proportion of their capital through borrowing. In the past the state guaranteed such borrowing, but this practice is now very rare, particularly in the context of Ireland's membership of the EU, where state supports are considered to be inimical to competition in the marketplace.

Even more so than for state agencies, identifying the appropriate degree of independence from central government for state enterprises is crucial to their successful performance. State enterprises are established to meet certain objectives and are expected to be entrepreneurial and innovative in achieving them, but they are also expected to use public funds prudently and operate subject to national interests. Their boards should contain persons who have extensive experience and knowledge of the commercial activity in question, and political interference in the decisions of the boards (such as increases in energy charges or closure of plants) tends to be avoided.

State enterprises are accountable to the Houses of the Oireachtas in a variety of ways. In the first instance, they must produce an annual report and accounts, copies of which are laid before the Houses. While they are removed from the day-to-day management, organisation and administration of state enterprises, ministers are expected to respond to any parliamentary questions concerning policies of state enterprises under their aegis. The enterprises are also accountable to various committees, and their chief executives may be called before the Committee of Public Accounts.

In 1976, in response to concerns that there was a deficit in public oversight of state enterprises, a joint committee on state-sponsored bodies was established to allow members of parliament to examine the work of the various enterprises. Though the reports of the committees tended not to be debated in the Dáil or Seanad, the committee provided an important link between elected members and the enterprises. Today, the responsibility is shared between the various committees shadowing government departments.

Like many of the state agencies discussed in Chapter 9, state enterprises are not staffed by civil servants and have their own systems of remuneration, evaluation and promotion. In fact, several of the older enterprises, including the ESB and CIÉ, have statutory power under their founding legislation to determine staff remuneration. Enterprises established more recently (particularly since the 1960s) require the consent of their minister when setting salary scales. Two pieces of legislation, the Worker Participation (State Enterprises) Acts 1977 and 1988, grant employees in certain state agencies and enterprises the right to have a representative on the board of directors. These bodies include FÁS, Bord Gáis, Bord na Móna, CIÉ, Coillte, ESB, An Post, RTÉ and Teagasc.

Unlike the practice in many other states, where one ministry or specially created state agency manages the state's duties as shareholder of several enterprises, in Ireland responsibility for each enterprise is often shared between the Department of Finance and another department. For example, the Department of Communications, Energy and Natural Resources has responsibility for some of the largest energy providers in the state. The Department of Finance has an interest in the performance of all enterprises given its role in ensuring co-ordination of national priorities and management of the state's finances. No enterprise may incur financial significant obligations without the prior permission of the Minister of Finance. Where an enterprise does so, it runs the risk of liquidation. For example, in 1984, having agreed to significant borrowings without the knowledge of the Minister for Finance, Irish Shipping closed down. The government refused to underwrite the costs arising from these unauthorised agreements.

Regulation

Today, many state enterprises compete with privately owned companies to provide energy, transport services such as buses, and television and radio services in both English and Irish. As many state enterprises have emerged from monopoly situations and could make it difficult for small private companies to compete with them, several 'regulators' have been established to ensure as level a playing field as possible for all through avoiding the dangers of monopoly. Therefore the Commission for Energy Regulation – the state agency responsible for regulating the communications sector – ensures that while the ESB may own the state's electricity supply infrastructure, it cannot unfairly prevent other electricity providers from using it. Similarly, the Commission for Aviation Regulation regulates airport charges at Dublin airport as well as service charges levied by the Irish Aviation Authority. These regulators fund their activities through levies imposed on the regulated enterprises. However, the balance between regulation and commercial freedom for state enterprises continues to be contested.

11

Financing the state

Delivering government and quality public services is an extremely costly exercise. So too is the development of the state's infrastructure. From the police and schools to roads and hospitals, there are myriad demands on the state's coffers at any one time, but governments cannot jeopardise the economy by borrowing too much money. Funding needs are almost always greater than available resources, and one of the key tasks of elected government is to decide on the manner in which resources are to be allocated. This is often a source of political conflict, as the public and their representatives are rarely in total agreement as to what the state should appropriately be involved in. As noted in Chapter 8, there has been increased emphasis in recent years on financial efficiency as part of the modernisation agenda as governments seek to achieve the maximum outputs for available input. However, not all government activity is easily measured, particularly in respect of its contribution to social development.

A government budget is a financial plan covering expenditure and receipts for a defined period of time. Usually, it is embodied in a document called 'the Budget', but the budget is much more than this. It is an important element in the financial and economic management of the state. Budgeting must, therefore, be regarded as much more than a routine book-keeping exercise; it involves politics, public administration and economics and has important social consequences. While the budget has grown over the past 40 years in line with the significant expansion of the public sector and the changing role played by the government in society, Ireland's recent rapid economic development has meant that the budget itself is a smaller, albeit crucial, portion of overall economic activity in the state.

As noted in Chapter 4, the Constitution explicitly gives the Dáil important duties in relation to approving financial legislation (Money Bills) and overseeing expenditure by the executive. Producing the annual budget is arguably the most important task of government and approving it one of the most important duties of the Dáil. Indeed, a government that cannot achieve Dáil approval for its budget may be expected to resign. The budget has three important functions.

1. Perhaps the most obvious role of the budget is that of *redistribution*. The budget will determine the taxation and welfare policies for the following year and the extent to which income is redistributed between rich and poor, across the regions and among generations.
2. The budget is also an exercise in *allocation*, i.e. expenditure must be allocated across the various functions of government, for example between health and education, and between consumption and investment.
3. The *stabilisation* role seeks to ensure sustained economic growth, low unemployment and low inflation. Also, the proportion of economic activity in a state that is created by government spending must not be too large in case it drives out private initiative, nor too small in case it contributes to economic decline.

Much of budget expenditure is difficult to change as it is committed to long-term projects or already 'earmarked' for new developments. However, even if much of government expenditure is irreversible or difficult to reduce in practical terms, there remain important decisions to be taken in the process of budget formulation.

As a member of the EU, Ireland ratified the Maastricht Treaty (see Chapter 19) in 1992. As well as providing a framework for the introduction of the euro currency, the subsequent Stability and Growth Pact committed Ireland to maintaining low levels of inflation as well as limiting the extent of borrowing that governments could undertake. Thus, when Ministers for Finance are drafting the budget, they must be cognisant of broader EU obligations as well as national ones.

By virtue of Article 11 of the Constitution, all revenues raised and collected by the state must be paid into the *Central Fund* (also known as the Exchequer), which is kept at the Central Bank. Every year, the Department of Finance is required to prepare accounts detailing funds going into and out of the Central Fund and to present them to the Dáil. These are called the *Finance Accounts* and are audited by the Comptroller and Auditor General.

Government income

Revenue is raised in Ireland through three main sources.

1. Tax revenue. A tax is a compulsory payment levied by a public authority. The following taxes are administered and collected by the Office of the Revenue Commissioners and paid over to the Exchequer Account at the Central Bank:

- income tax
- customs tax
- corporation tax
- estate duties
- value-added tax (VAT)
- residential property tax
- agricultural levies
- capital taxes
- employment and training levy
- stamp duties.

It should be noted that income tax, VAT, excise duties and corporation tax contribute over 90% of the total revenue. Motor taxes (and driving licence fees) are collected by local authorities and are paid into the Local Government Fund.[28]

2. Non-tax revenue. The main items of non-tax revenue that are lodged with the Exchequer include:

- surplus income of the Central Bank
- proceeds of National Lottery surplus
- interest on Exchequer advances to state agencies and enterprises
- dividends on shares held for the benefit of the Minister for Finance (on behalf of the Exchequer) in state enterprises and other companies
- royalties
- fees (e.g. court fees, companies' registration fees, passport and consular fees, property registry fees)
- EU refunds.

---

[28] There are a number of other funds into which levies are channelled but which do not go through the Exchequer Account, including the health, employment and education funds.

3. Non-revenue or capital receipts include:

- EU Structural Funds[29] (see also Chapter 19)
- proceeds of sales of shares held for the benefit of the Minister for Finance
- proceeds from the sale of state property.

With the agreement of the Minister for Finance, the National Treasury Management Agency (see below) may also borrow money on behalf of the state. No other minister has authority to borrow money without the approval of the Minister for Finance.

Government spending takes two forms:

- *capital spending* involves the use of resources to develop the state's assets, such as school buildings or roads
- *current expenditure* is the cost of maintaining those assets annually, as well as public service salaries and social welfare benefits for citizens.

The Constitution provides that the government must seek the approval of the Dáil for most of its spending (capital and current) plans. This is known as *voted expenditure* as a vote normally takes place to approve the plans, and the government is accountable to the Dáil for the appropriate use of those funds. The Dáil cannot approve the use of funds unless they are proposed to it by the government and signed by the Minister for Finance. There is also *non-voted expenditure* which, as the name suggests, does not require Dáil approval and which is for the purposes of issues such as the payment of interest on the national debt.

In general, there is broad consensus among Irish people that the state should provide health, education and social welfare services. Hence they account for large portions of the annual budget in terms of current spending (over 75% in Budget 2008).

---

[29] In 2007 Ireland received almost €2 billion in funding from the EU, and contributed €1.5 billion. By 2013 Ireland is expected to be a net contributor to the EU, giving approximately €500 million more than it receives.

The annual financial cycle

The framework for managing public finances is set out in the 'Public Financial Procedures'[30] (or Blue Book). This also details the annual financial timetable, which has two main phases that can be referred to as the formulation and implementation phases. They can be summarised as follows.

Budget formulation

February
The Department of Finance requests all other departments to submit their projections of spending for the next three years. In order to do this, a 'No Policy Change' (NPC) scenario is adopted which implies that the projections reflect the continuation of the existing level of service.

March/April
The departments begin the process of developing their economic forecasts for the following year. They submit their projections and initial discussion take place between each department and the Department of Finance concerning the figures.

May/June
Based on these figures, as well as consideration of the wider EU and international growth predictions, the Minister for Finance prepares a *Budgetary Strategy Memorandum* (BSM) for the government, setting out the Department of Finance's assessment of the budgetary and economic outlook into the medium term. In this context, the Department of Finance reviews the current year and prepares projections of revenues and of expenditure involved in maintaining the existing levels of public services for each of the three subsequent years. On foot of the BSM, the government approves targets for the main budgetary aggregates including borrowing, deficits, changes to expenditure and taxation levels.

Based on these broad considerations, the Department of Finance prepares the annual Estimates Circular and sends it to departments. The circular explains to the departments the parameters within which they should prepare their detailed estimates for the following year's Budget, as well as the two years after that. These may require departments to

---

[30] Available at www.finance.gov.ie

reduce spending in some areas in order to ensure that overall national targets are met.

July/September

In response to the Estimates Circular, the departments revise their economic forecasts and submit draft estimates to the Department of Finance for examination. In advance of doing so, departments may consider submissions received from interest groups and other organisations that will normally appeal for funding increases for their work. Once the draft estimates have been received, the Department of Finance holds detailed discussions with each department on its figures to ensure that they are in line with the stipulations of the circular. If any areas remain unresolved, the Department of Finance informs the government and the relevant ministers must come to an agreement. The department also submits a BSM to government which, if agreed, sets the overall budgetary framework. At the end of this part of the process, therefore, there will be a government decision approving detailed expenditure of departments (and some central government agencies) for the next financial year in question, as well as financial envelopes for the following two years.

October/November

Prior to 2007, a document known as the *Abridged Estimates Volume* (AEV) was produced in which spending plans would be outlined. The AEV was also an accounting and control document as it allowed for comparison between the estimated and actual budget for the previous year. Other historical data were provided for comparative purposes.

In 2007, a new development in the budgetary process occurred with the publication in October of the *Pre-Budget Outlook* (PBO). Apart from considering economic and fiscal projection for the three years ahead, the PBO details the money needed to maintain current levels of public service given inflation and other pressures. The introduction of the PBO is to allow for a more informed debate on new measures announced on Budget Day by providing more information on existing spending levels. Under the previous system, new expenditure initiatives were announced not only in the Budget but also in the AEV and the *Revised Estimates Volume* (see below). Instead, new spending and taxation plans are now held back until Budget Day, when they can be announced. During this period, some ministers may hold pre-budget forums with relevant groups to present information and hear views. In the light of these discussions, the Minister for Finance formulates proposals for adjustments to the pre-Budget Estimate allocations for the next three years and brings these proposals to government for approval.

December

The weekend before the actual Budget is produced, the *White Paper on Receipts and Expenditure* is published. The White Paper presents high-level figures concerning the previous financial year, and estimates for receipts from tax and expenditure for the year ahead (in the absence of any changes on Budget Day), as well as any borrowing requirements. The White Paper is not debated in the Dáil but provokes much speculation in the media about the ensuing budget and what it may contain. The overall surplus/deficit in the budget figures at this stage gives a preliminary indication as regards the scope for cuts in taxation or increases in public expenditure.

The Minister for Finance presents the Budget to the Dáil (usually on the first Wednesday in December) in what is referred to as his *Financial Statement*. In it, the minister sets out the government's assessment of economic prospects for the year ahead, details tax changes and outlines all new expenditure decisions. Reforms introduced in 2007 mean that key announcements on spending and income are now made together. New spending decisions normally include provisions for public service pay and increases in social welfare rates. The *Budget Book* is published on Budget Day (in recent years it has also appeared in a CD format). It normally contains:

- the full text of the Budget speech as delivered in the Dáil
- a number of explanatory tables
- principal features of the Budget and accompanying tables highlighting the likely effects on the individual's tax liability, entitlement to social welfare benefits, etc.
- the financial resolutions required to give immediate effect to any tax changes proposed in the budget pending the passing of the Finance Act (e.g. changes in excise rates)
- the update to the Stability Programme (required by the EU)
- the previously published White Paper on Receipts and Expenditure
- estimates of the consolidated capital and current accounts of the Exchequer and the various extra-budgetary funds classified according to the definitions used in national income accounting.

After the Minister for Finance has finished presenting the Budget speech to the Dáil and the Opposition spokesperson on Finance has replied briefly, the minister introduces what are called the *Financial Resolutions*. They are dealt with at once and cover any new taxes, any increase in existing tax, any variation in a temporary tax or any removal of a temporary tax. These specific resolutions are debated on the night of the Budget and, when passed, allow immediate collection of any taxes imposed or varied depending on the enactment of the Finance Bill. The resolutions usually relate to increases in excise duties.

All the expenditure adjustments to the pre-Budget Estimates are published in a *Budget Estimates Volume (*BEV). The BEV also includes a Summary Public Capital Programme and shows the amount of capital carryover in line with the Multi-Annual Capital Envelope framework.

In late December, the annual Appropriation Act is passed giving statutory effect to the Estimates, including any Supplementary Estimates, voted by the Dáil for the current year. The Act also serves a number of other important functions, including the provision of a basis for expenditure to continue to take place in the next year before the Estimates for that year have passed. In this regard, before the end of December the Statement of Authorised Issues in respect of the following year is laid before the Dáil.

Budget Implementation

February

The annual *Finance Bill* is published and referred to the Dáil. After debate has concluded on the Finance Bill, it is enacted into law. The Bill must be signed by the President within four months of Budget Day. From this period onwards, attention switches to its implementation. This Bill gives legislative effect to the tax changes proposed in the Budget Statement and to other detailed taxation measures deemed necessary. The *Revised Estimates Volume* for the year is also published in February, along with the Public Capital Programme. The individual Estimates are referred by the Dáil to their relevant Select Committees for consideration, together with the *Annual Output Statements* (see *Budgetary oversight* below), after which the Dáil votes on the individual spending Estimates. The Dáil approves the Estimates by way of *Financial Resolutions*. Before the Dáil has approved the Estimates, expenditure in that year on existing services is authorised under the provisions of the 1965 Central Fund (Permanent Provisions) Act. Also, a Social Welfare Bill is initiated in order to give immediate effect to the social welfare provisions in the Budget.

June–December
If during the course of the latter half of the year additional moneys are required by departments to meet their commitments, *Supplementary Estimates* must be submitted to the Dáil for approval.

December
The final significant stage in the financial cycle is the *Appropriation Bill*. It is passed by the Dáil when consideration of all the departmental estimates has been finalised and is usually one of the last items of legislative business of the financial year. The Act appropriates to the particular services the sums voted by the Dáil in the interval since the previous year's Act (including the Supplementary Estimates).

Budgetary oversight

As described in Chapter 8, the Sectoral Policy Division of the Department of Finance plays an important role in the management and co-ordination of the annual financial cycle. Spending is monitored on a monthly basis and Exchequer Statements are presented to government to highlight any divergence from the stipulations of the budget. Also, a press conference is normally held at the end of every quarter of the year to provide information on national finances. However, at the end of each financial year (December) each department prepares an *Appropriation Account* which acts as an audit of the budget. The account presents actual spending and receipts against the figures provided for in the Estimates, as well as other details such as a statement of assets and liabilities.

A new development announced in Budget 2007 concerns departmental *Annual Output Statements* which represent a further development in the efforts to provide better information on the outcomes of government expenditure in different policy areas. The scheme was piloted initially in a number of departments for Budget 2008. All departments must now produce them and they are presented to the relevant Oireachtas committee along with the estimates for the year ahead. Each statement will identify what outputs the department achieved with its budget and what its output aims are for the year ahead.

As part of the process of financial accountability, Accounting Officers must 'sign off' on the account for the vote for their department or office. They must also send their accounts to the Comptroller and Auditor General.

The Comptroller and Auditor General

Established upon independence in 1922,[31] the Comptroller and Auditor General is one of only three officers specifically named in the 1937 Constitution of Ireland – the other two being the President and the Attorney General. Though traditionally the least well known of these three constitutional offices, in the past ten years or so the work of the Comptroller and Auditor General has become more familiar to the general public through the publication of high-profile reports of audits and examinations.

In order to ensure the office's impartiality, the Comptroller and Auditor General is independent of both the government and the Houses of the Oireachtas, though the office has a special relationship with the Committee of Public Accounts (see below). The office-holder is appointed by the President on the nomination of the Dáil. As an extension of this autonomy, the Comptroller and Auditor General is also independent of all the public bodies audited by him/her. To safeguard the policy-making role of the executive, the Comptroller and Auditor General cannot comment on or criticise government policy. However, in the course of his/her audits and examinations, the Comptroller and Auditor General is entitled to examine and report on the implementation or results of policy decisions.

At present, the Comptroller and Auditor General audits the accounts of almost 400 public bodies, including:

* government departments and offices
* departmental funds (such as the Social Insurance Fund)
* health-related organisations and agencies (including public hospitals)
* educational bodies (such as Vocational Education Committees, Institutes of Technology and universities)
* state agencies
* cross-border bodies.[32]

The Comptroller and Auditor General has no power to audit democratically elected local authorities. Instead, the Local Government Audit Service of the Department of the Environment, Heritage and Local Government carries out this duty.

---

[31] Articles 62 and 63 of the 1922 Irish Free State Constitution provided for the office's establishment.

[32] This work is performed in collaboration with the Northern Ireland Audit Office.

Article 33 defines the two roles of the Comptroller and Auditor General, as follows.

The Comptroller General role – 'to control on behalf of the State all disbursements'
This role relates to the control of funds released from the Exchequer as agreed by the Dáil. In effect it is an independent check that money is made available to the government only to the extent authorised by Dáil Éireann. The process starts when the Minister for Finance (or the National Treasury Management Agency – see below) requisitions a specific sum of money in writing. When the Comptroller and Auditor General is satisfied that the sum is authorised by law and that no specified limits are exceeded, he/she authorises the release of the requested funds in writing.

The Auditor General role – 'to audit all accounts of moneys administered by or under the authority of the Oireachtas'
This role encompasses a number of functions, which can be summarised as accuracy, regularity, inspections, value for money and probity.

The *accuracy* function relates to the accounts of the audited organisation and ensuring that they reflect the financial transactions undertaken by the organisation. *Regularity* refers to the duty of organisations to use funds for the purposes intended and in accordance with any relevant rules and regulations. As well as audits, the Comptroller and Auditor General is empowered to inspect the records of bodies that receive more than half of their funding directly or indirectly from the state. This *inspection* role is a more restricted examination than a full financial audit. *Probity* refers to the proper conduct of public business and involves fair and ethical behaviour, as well as the avoidance of potential conflicts of interest. Compliance with tax laws is also a key element of probity. Finally, public organisations are required to achieve *value for money* (VFM) when using their funds. VFM audits seek to identify that public bodies are being economic, efficient and effective (the three 'E's) in carrying out their functions. VFM audits encourage the various parts of the public sector to seek to achieve 'more from less'. The Comptroller and Auditor General (Amendment) Act 1993 (see below) provides a statutory basis for VFM examinations.

The three 'E's that constitute the VFM audits can be summarised as follows.

- *Economy:* Getting the right quality and quantity of inputs at the best price.
- *Efficiency:* Minimising the inputs if the outputs are fixed or maximising the outputs if the inputs are fixed.
- *Effectiveness:* Whether or not adequate systems are in place to monitor the use of funds.

One of the main functions of the Comptroller and Auditor General as outlined in Article 33 of the Constitution is to report his/her work to Dáil Éireann and, by extension, to the general public. The Comptroller and Auditor General produces several financial reports as part of the process of ensuring financial accountability of the public administration.

All financial audits result in an *audit certificate* in which the Comptroller and Auditor General expresses an opinion on the accounts of the organisation being audited.

Supplements to audit certificates may also be supplied in respect of audits outside of central government departments and offices.

The Comptroller and Auditor General's *Annual Report on the Appropriation Accounts* is an important part of the Annual Financial Cycle. Rather than detailing all the work undertaken over the previous 12 months, the Annual Report identifies any significant issues arising out of the audits or on foot of specific investigations. The Annual Report also contains the audited Appropriation Accounts of government departments and offices.

Finally, the Comptroller and Auditor General has the power to produce special reports on matters that justify a more in-depth examination, particularly in relation to VFM issues.

The Comptroller and Auditor General (Amendment) Act 1993

This Act provides the main legislative basis for the work of the Comptroller and Auditor General. It consolidates previous legislation and confers new statutory functions on the Comptroller and Auditor General. Importantly, the Act sets out the duties of Accounting Officers of audited bodies: they are responsible to Dáil Éireann for the proper expenditure of money granted to those bodies. Other main provisions of this Act are:

- the conducting of VFM examinations of all bodies audited by the Comptroller and Auditor General

- the extension of the remit of the Comptroller and Auditor General to new areas, including organisations in the health and education sectors
- allowing for the inspection of bodies that have more than half of their funding from the state
- ensuring that access is provided to required records
- providing for the audit of the Office of the Comptroller and Auditor General by independent auditors.

The Committee of Public Accounts
The Dáil Committee of Public Accounts (or Public Accounts Committee, PAC) comprises 12 TDs, none of whom may be a member of the government or a minister of state. By convention, the chairperson of the committee is a member of the Opposition. The Comptroller and Auditor General is not a member of the committee but always attends its meetings as a 'permanent witness', and the reports from his/her office form the basis for the committee's work. The committee is one of the longest existing in the Oireachtas and has developed a reputation for the non-partisan nature of its work. Reflecting this, very few votes are taken in the committee and members proceed by consensus rather than according to party political lines.

The committee meets weekly and has the power to send for persons, papers and records. Accounting Officers of public organisations from government departments to state agencies can be called to appear before the PAC to answer questions. The committee may suggest topics or issues for examination by the Comptroller and Auditor General, but the latter retains the discretion as to whether or not to act on these suggestions.

National Treasury Management Agency
In 1990 the government passed the National Treasury Management Agency Act, which delegated the Minister for Finance's borrowing and debt management functions to a new and independent agency subject to the minister's guidance. While the minister remains responsible for policy in relation to the management of the debt and related borrowings, and is accountable to the Dáil in this regard, the National Treasury Management Agency (NTMA) administers the state's debts.

The success of the NTMA in reducing the state's debts has seen extra functions conferred on it in recent years, and other agencies under its remit include:

- the National Pensions Reserve Fund Commission, which is responsible for managing a fund to which the state contributes 1% of GNP annually in order to fund future pensions liabilities
- the National Development Finance Agency (NDFA), which advises on and raises money on behalf of public bodies delivering infrastructure projects. The NDFA is also deeply involved in organising public–private partnerships for the delivery of such projects.

Central Bank and Irish Financial Services Regulatory Authority

Originally established in 1943, in 2003 the Central Bank was changed into the Central Bank and Irish Financial Services Regulatory Authority following Ireland's entry to the euro currency area. While the Central Bank retained its principal function of acting as the state's banker and is responsible for the printing of money, a new and independent financial regulator was created to oversee the work of all financial institutions in the state.

12

Local government and administration

Very few states are administered by only one tier of government. In order to fulfil the democratic requirement that citizens must be able to take responsibility for matters directly affecting them, it is often necessary to create different levels of government, each with its own set of powers and areas of concern. Apart from central or federal government, state, regional, city, county, municipal, town or even district governments may exist, each with representatives elected by the people to run them.

In Ireland, the only other level of democratically appointed government is local government. It consists of county, city and town councils (local authorities), whose existence actually pre-dates the state's foundation. The 1898 Local Government (Ireland) Act provided for the rationalisation of local authority structures and functions, and established a local government system based on counties as the principal units. More recently, and in line with other EU member states, some regional-level administration has emerged (see below).

Apart from the Dáil and the Presidency, local authorities are the only entities directly elected by the people in the state. An insertion to the Constitution in 1999 provided for elections every five years to local authorities, which provide 'a forum for the democratic representation of local communities, in exercising and performing at local level powers and functions conferred by law and in promoting by its initiatives the interests of such communities' (Article 28A).

The structure of local government

The component parts of local government are as follows.

- *29 county[33] and five city[34] councils.* The 2001 Local Government Act describes them as the 'primary units of local government', and city and county councils perform similar functions. Combined they cover the entire area of the Republic of Ireland.
- *75 town and five borough[35] councils.* These smaller units exist within county council areas and their status as local authorities stems from their historical existence as large towns. There is considerable variation in the powers held by these authorities, with some (particularly the borough councils) maintaining a wide range of functions and others few, having devolved most of them upwards to the county council. However, many new towns, particularly around Dublin where the population has expanded significantly, do not have such councils.

Each of these local authorities has an elected council, ranging from nine politicians or 'members' to 52. The total number of local councillors in the state is 1,627.

Councillors

As with members of Dáil Éireann, councillors are elected by PR-STV on a five-year basis. Unlike Dáil Éireann, local councils tend to run their full term and councillors do not dissolve their council early or call new elections. Also, candidates and voters for local government do not have to be Irish citizens. When they occur, local elections are as competitive as their national counterparts, with candidates often facing competition for seats from within their own party as well as from other quarters. Each constituency is subdivided into a number of local electoral areas. Once elected, councils normally meet once a month but the majority of councillors are also appointed to various committees and bodies operating at local and regional level (see below). The Local Government Act of 2001 abolished the 'dual mandate', and since 2004 no councillor can also hold a seat in the Oireachtas.

---

[33] Although the Republic of Ireland consists of 26 counties, there are 29 county councils. For historical reasons, Tipperary has two county councils – North Tipperary and South Tipperary – while the area of the former Dublin County Council now consists of Fingal, South Dublin and Dun Laoghaire-Rathdown County Councils.

[34] Dublin, Cork, Galway, Limerick, Waterford.

[35] Drogheda, Clonmel, Wexford, Sligo, Kilkenny. They were originally established as 'borough corporations' and have a larger number of elected members (12) than most, but not all, town councils.

Almost all councillors are aligned to national political parties. They therefore have a dual loyalty – primarily to their local communities as elected representatives but also to their political parties for which they are the local champions. Local politics in Ireland does not always follow the pattern of national politics, and novel coalitions of parties can be found throughout the local government system (though the coalitions tend to exist for the purposes of holding offices such as mayor). There are 970 elected members of city and county councils and they form the bulk of the electorate for 43 panel seats in Seanad Éireann (see Chapter 5). Since 2002, city and county councillors are paid a salary equivalent to a quarter of a senator's annual salary; a smaller salary is paid to councillors for borough and town councils.

Functions of local government

Local government in Ireland performs many different roles – embodiment of democracy, service provider, local regulator but also an important element of the executive apparatus of state.[36] However, when compared to systems of local government in other EU states, the Irish system can be regarded as one of the more centralised, with many local services such as policing, education and health controlled and administered by the government departments and their various regional offices. Indeed, many citizens associate local government principally with activities relating to the physical environment such as roads and parks. This centralisation is also evident in relation to funding, and the absence of a comprehensive system of local taxation determines that local authorities are reliant on the Exchequer to fund many of their activities. In most other EU states, local authorities are involved in delivering a greater range of services, and paying local taxes for these services is a normal part of life for citizens.

While the multitude of services provided by local authorities is too often forgotten, it is also forgotten that most of these activities are determined by central government through statute. In other words, the functions that local authorities perform are given to them through legislation enacted by the Oireachtas. In doing this, the Oireachtas frequently imposes a duty on a minister (usually the Minister for

---

[36] Callanan, M. (2003) 'The Role of Local Government', in M. Callanan and J. Keogan (eds), *Local Government in Ireland: Inside Out.* Dublin: Institute of Public Administration, pp. 3–13.

Environment, Heritage and Local Government) to supervise some aspects of how they implement the legislation. The range of activities performed at this level arise from what Roche summarises as 'history, accident [and] tradition',[37] rather than solely through an agreed division of labour with central government. Local authority functions or services are traditionally grouped around eight subject headings, known as the 'programme groups'. The eight programme groups are as follows.

Programme Group 1: Housing and building

These functions include the management and provision of social housing, addressing problems of homelessness, the provision of housing for the travelling community and the enforcement of a regulatory regime at local level to maintain housing standards and controls. County councils, city councils, borough councils and most town councils are normally the appropriate 'housing authority'[38] within their functional area.

Programme Group 2: Roads and transportation

As part of the work in this programme, local authorities are involved in road development and maintenance, vehicle and driver licensing, public lighting and traffic management. Local authorities also work with the National Roads Authority (NRA) in the delivery of national roads. As of 2008, responsibility for non-national roads (i.e. local country roads) shifted from the Department of the Environment, Heritage and Local Government to the Department of Transport.

Programme Group 3: Water and sewerage

The county and city councils are 'water services authorities', and are charged with providing public water supplies, wastewater treatment, and financial and other supports to private householders and to groups supplying such facilities. The EU has also played a significant role in the development of water standards, treatment and infrastructure. In 2003 the county councils assumed the sanitary functions of town and borough councils in their area.

---

[37] Roche, D. (1982) *Local Government in Ireland.* Dublin: Institute of Public Administration, p. 7.

[38] A convention in the drafting of legislation is to refer to groups of local authorities (e.g. city and county councils alone, or town and borough councils only) as authorities for certain functions, such as 'sanitary authorities', 'roads authorities' or 'planning authorities'.

Programme Group 4: Planning and development
Another role performed by local authorities is that of planning authorities. This includes physical planning policy, the control and development of buildings, provision and facilitation of economic and social development, and planning enforcement. The local authorities have primary responsibility for approving (or preventing) development within their territory, and many urban and village renewal projects have been undertaken by local authorities in this respect.

Work in this area is largely framed by the City/County Development Plan that the law requires planning authorities to develop every five years. Under planning legislation such as the various Local Government (Planning and Development) Acts, Development Plans must provide for:

• the 'zoning' of land for different uses, e.g. housing, farming, public amenities, industry
• traffic management
• the redevelopment of obsolete areas
• the preservation and improvement of areas and amenities.

There is an appeals mechanism for local authority planning decisions to an independent state agency called An Bord Pleanála. Planning is perhaps the most controversial of all the services provided by councils.

Programme Group 5: Environmental protection
This programme includes waste collection, fire protection and prevention, pollution control and building safety and is consuming an ever-increasing portion of local authority resources. In particular, waste management has become a contentious issue as local authorities attempt to meet the costs of dealing with large volumes of waste and adhering to increasingly stringent environmental standards. As well as waste management, litter and water pollution, this programme includes expenditure on civil defence and the fire services. Local authorities collectively manage 37 fire authorities which are responsible for over 220 fire stations through the state. The fire services are provided by a combination of full-time professional and part-time firefighters. In Dublin, the fire services also provide an ambulance service.

Programme Group 6: Recreation and amenity
There have been considerable developments under this programme as local authorities have become increasingly involved in activities

relating to social development. Work includes the provision of libraries, swimming pools, parks, open spaces, recreation centres, museums, galleries and other public amenities. Arts initiatives are also common, and many councils now have an Arts Officer.

Programme Group 7: Agriculture, education, health and welfare

Before 1970, when regional Health Boards were established, this was one of the most important areas of activity for local authorities due to their involvement in local health issues. Today, local authority involvement in health matters is minor and contributions to the education sector consist mainly of making nominations to Vocational Education Committees (see below) or the distribution of higher education grants provided by the Department of Education and Science. Other aspects of the programme include veterinary services.

Programme Group 8: Miscellaneous services

This programme covers all remaining services provided by local authorities, including:

- the maintenance of the register of electors
- the provision of animal pounds and collection of wandering animals
- the provision of coroners and inquests
- publication of reports and auditing of financial accounts.

As well as these eight programme groups, a recent addition is the contribution of local authorities to the co-ordination of 'community and enterprise' activities, which has seen them become more involved (alongside City and County Development Boards – see below) with tackling the difficult issue of social exclusion.

Financing local government

In terms of capital expenditure for the development of infrastructure and other assets, local authorities rely mainly on state grants. However, subject to approval from central government, they may also borrow money or generate internal capital receipts through, for example, the sale of property or more recently through development levies imposed as part of the granting of planning permission.

In terms of current expenditure, local authorities raise funds through a variety of mechanisms, as follows (see Figure 12.1).

1. State grants for specific projects carried out on behalf of the state, such as national roads.
2. Charges for services, such as social housing rents, refuse charges, commercial water charges, and planning application or driver licence fees.
3. Commercial rates, which are levied on businesses in a local authority area. The level of this rate is determined each year as part of the local authority's annual budgetary process.
4. Money from the Local Government Fund, which was established in 1998. This is an account into which all proceeds from motor taxation go, as well as an annual sum of money from central government. A 'needs and resources' equalisation model is used to help distribute funds across local authorities according to a range of factors including population, geographical size and existing infrastructure, as well as where needs are greater than projected resources.

In 2006 local authorities sourced some 57% of current expenditure from their own sources (commercial rates 27%; goods and services 30%), the remainder being provided by way of government grants/subsidies (23%) and general-purpose grants from the Local Government Fund (20%). For most local authorities, the Local Government Fund and grants are key sources of revenue for capital and current expenditure, with fees and charges also contributing a significant portion of income.

Figure 12.1. *Sources of local authority current expenditure, 2006 (%)*

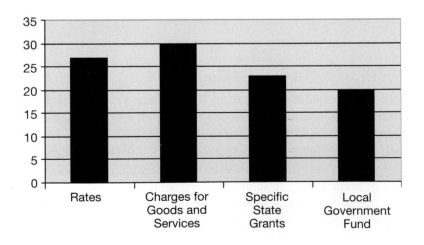

An unusual feature of Irish local government is that tax on property exists for buildings used for commercial purposes only, with the value of those buildings being established by the Valuation Office. The burden of rates for domestic dwellings was removed from homeowners in 1978, and rates on agricultural land were subsequently declared unconstitutional by the courts in 1982. Several subsequent reports on local government financing have identified the absence of local taxation as contributing to a disjoint between taxes paid to central government and services provided locally to citizens. It has also led to difficulties in respect of the introduction of charges for increasingly expensive services such as waste management, or for new houses through the development contribution levy.

Decision-making at the local level

At national government level in Ireland, elected politicians (and particularly ministers) retain the sole power of decision-making across all aspects of policy. At local government level, however, there is a formal separation of powers between the elected councillors and the most senior administrator in the council – the City or County Manager. The distinction is made by decisions being referred to as either *reserved functions* or *executive functions*, which are set out clearly in the legislation governing all the specific functions of local government. The former decisions are so called as they are reserved for elected members to decide (by majority vote if necessary); the latter are controlled by the executive or administrative arm of the council.

Since the introduction of the system of city (and later county) management in the period 1929–1942, managers have developed both formal and informal powers within local authorities. They are not elected but instead are normally approved by the council for a period of seven years following a recommendation by the Public Appointments Service, which interviews and selects candidates. Today, the Local Government Act of 2001 and subsequent legislation has detailed the division of powers, and any function not designated as a reserved function in law is automatically deemed to be an executive one.

Reserved functions tend to be those establishing the parameters of policy as well as oversight of the work of the local authority itself, for example:

- adopting the annual local authority budget
- making or revoking by-laws (a form of secondary legislation)
- adopting a development plan for the local authority area
- inspecting decisions made by the manager and his or her staff.

The County or City Manager and his/her staff must operate within the policy framework set down by the elected representatives as well as legislation passed by the Oireachtas. Managers' more important decisions are made by way of signed *Manager's Orders*, which are legal documents. Examples of executive functions include:

- decisions concerning the granting or withholding of planning permission
- hiring and firing of local authority staff
- allocation of social houses.

While the distinction between reserved and executive functions is an essential feature of local authority work, in reality there is close co-operation between the administrative and elected arms of city and county councils. The key link between the two arms is the relationship between manager and the chairperson (the Mayor or Cathaoirleach) of the council, who is elected annually by the council. Given that most local councillors are employed in other capacities, they tend to rely heavily on the work and advice of officials, particularly in relation to detailed matters or the legal boundaries of local authority work.

Reform of local government

Calls for local government reform have frequently been made since the state's foundation. A common theme of reform proposals has been the need for devolution of responsibility from central to local government. It is only since the 1990s that substantial and sustained reform has been undertaken across a range of policy and internal management issues, and the roots for these developments are to be found in the broad principles of the Strategic Management Initiative (Chapter 8). The reform programme for local government was called *Better Local Government – A Programme for Change* (BLG). BLG established four key principles, some of which were reflective of changes within the civil service under the other SMI-inspired programme, *Delivering Better Government* (Chapter 8; see Table 12.1).

A number of initiatives occurred under each of the four principles, as follows.

Table 12.1. *Main features of local government and central government (civil service) reform*

Better Local Government	Delivering Better Government
• Enhancing local democracy and widening participation • Serving the customer better • Developing efficiency • Provision of proper resources	• Devolution of authority and accountability • Quality customer service • Strategic planning • Performance and financial management

Enhancing local democracy and widening participation
- The provision of constitutional recognition for local government.
- The establishment of Area Committees to oversee service delivery within each local authority.
- The establishment of Strategic Policy Committees (see below).
- Closer integration of local development with local government (through the creation of City and County Development Boards – see below).

Serving the customer better
- Development of 42 key performance indicators for all local authorities.
- Creation of 'one-stop shops' for the public to access services.
- Better public access to information.
- Greater emphasis on the delivery of quality services.

Developing efficiency
- Introduction of value-for-money audits.
- Devolution of personnel management to the local authorities.
- Creation of a new management tier – the Director of Service – to support SPCs and oversee service provision.

Provision of proper resources
- Creation of the Local Government Fund.
- 'Ring-fencing' of proceeds of motor tax for the Local Government Fund.

Strategic Policy Committees and Corporate Policy Groups

While the elected council remains the principal decision-making body at local level, the establishment of Strategic Policy Committees (SPCs) as part of the reform agenda helps improve the quality of information being placed before the Councils. First established in 1998–9, SPCs are in effect sub-committees of the Council and help it to develop its policies in various areas. They have an advisory role only. Each city and county council was given the freedom to choose the number of SPCs it wanted and the policy areas covered by each, for example transport, environment and community and enterprise. Each SPC has a membership comprising two-thirds elected members and one-third 'sectoral interests', i.e. representatives from local business associations, community and voluntary organisations, environmental groups, trade unions, and farming bodies. The chair of the SPC must be a member of the council.

SPCs allow for more detailed discussion of new policies, plans and by-laws between public representatives and involved interests. In theory at least, the engagement of 'stakeholders' in policy formulation improves the quality of proposals and increases the likelihood of their acceptance at the implementation stage. Recommendations from SPCs are forwarded to the full council, where final decisions are taken. Each SPC is supported by a *Director of Service*. These positions were introduced in 2002 in order to provide a more strategic approach to local authority work. Each director has delegated management responsibility for specific service areas, and the number of directors varies between local authorities. The Directors of Service and the manager make up the senior management team of the local authority.

Another important institutional innovation in local authorities has been the creation of Corporate Policy Groups (CPGs). The CPG consists of the chairs of the SPCs as well as the Mayor or Cathaoirleach. The CPG co-ordinates the work of the SPCs before presenting final policy recommendations to the council. Other duties include the development of five-year corporate plans and the preparation of the annual budget. The manager normally supports the work of the CPG and attends its meetings (see Figure 12.2).

As local government develops, new mechanisms and structures continue to be created in order to ensure local authority input into various emerging issues. For example, these might include the evolving Joint Policing Committees (see Chapter 16), the River Basin Advisory

Figure 12.2. *SPCs, CPG and the council: path of policy proposals*

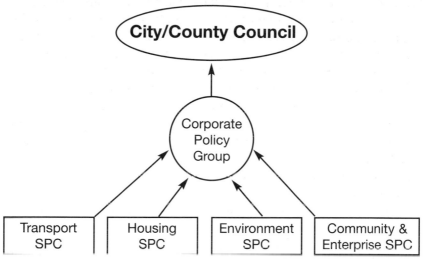

Councils and consultative Regional Health Fora. Local authorities are also formally represented on a range of local and regional bodies that are considered below.

Local and regional agencies

As well as democratically elected local authorities, there are over 250 bodies delivering, regulating and co-ordinating services at the sub national level in Ireland. The categories of organisation and a brief description of the role and composition of each are given below, beginning with those operating at local level.

Harbour commissions[39]

Harbour commissions (also known as harbour authorities) are elected in the same year as local authorities and consist of representatives of stakeholders including harbour users and local authorities, as well as ministerial appointees. These individuals are known as commissioners, and each harbour authority also has a Harbour Master. Since 2006, the 10 harbour commissions (and two harbour authorities[40]) are the responsibility of the Department of Transport. As the name suggests,

---

[39] Harbour commissions should be distinguished from port companies, which are commercial enterprises (see Chapter 10).
[40] Youghal and Kilrush.

harbour commissions administer and run harbours in various locations; they partially fund their activities through the collection of rates and charges (such as berthing fees), as well as departmental grants.

Some of the harbours are very small and are managed by an individual Harbour Master on a part-time basis, whereas others employ several staff. While the 1946 Harbours Act is still the principal governing legislation for the commissions, the government published its 'Ports Policy Statement' in 2005, which envisages the eventual transfer of harbour authority administration to local authorities or port companies.

City and county enterprise boards

Enterprise boards were first established in 1993 to encourage local enterprise and entrepreneurship, particularly in the areas of manufacturing, services and tourism. Their creation was supported by money provided from the EU for regional development. The Industrial Development Act, 1995 provided legal recognition for them as companies limited by guarantee. There are 35 enterprise boards in total and, with the exception of Co. Cork, their areas of operation are consistent with local authority boundaries. The function of enterprise boards is to help establish and thereafter support the development of employment and training through small enterprises, i.e. businesses employing fewer than 10 people. This ranges from support in business planning to financial assistance. Each enterprise board has a chief executive officer and a small number of staff.

The composition of each board is described in its Articles and Memorandum of Association. Normally, the boards consist of an independent chairperson and 14 ordinary members. Of the 14, four are local authority elected members and they are joined by representatives from state organisations (such as FÁS), the social partners (i.e. trade unions, employers, farming, and community and voluntary sectors) and local business or development organisations.

Partnerships

Also known as area partnerships or partnership companies, partnerships were established during the 1991–6 period in areas of disadvantage and high unemployment as independent companies limited by guarantee. They were modelled on the highly successful social partnership arrangements at national level (Chapter 8). Their work is mainly focused on issues of social inclusion and community development. Their creation was designed to help adapt national policies on these issues to local circumstances and need. As with enterprise boards, each has a Memorandum and Articles of Association, and EU funding played an important role in their establishment.

Partnerships do not follow local authority boundaries, and by 2007 there were 38 in existence. Each has a board of directors consisting of local authority members, representatives of the social partners, various state organisations and community and voluntary organisations active in economic and social development. Funding for the work of partnerships comes from central government via a state agency with charitable status known as *Pobal*. Partnerships range in size from those with fewer than 10 staff to those with as many as 70. Several partnerships are involved in the delivery of other programmes such as LEADER groups (see below); at the time of writing efforts are being made to provide where possible mergers between those partnerships and LEADER groups working within or across similar local authority boundaries. This is known as the 'cohesion process' and is being overseen by the Department of Community, Rural and Gaeltacht Affairs.

LEADER groups

LEADER is an acronym for *Liaisons Entre Actions de Développement de l'Économie Rurale* (Links between Development Actions for the Rural Economy). It is an EU-sponsored initiative created to foster rural development at the local level through 'groups', and LEADER groups are in existence in many other EU member states. In Ireland, 17 groups were established in 1991 under LEADER I. LEADER II spanned the period 1994–9 and the number of groups expanded to 34; there were also a number of sectoral bodies.[41] LEADER+ covered the period 2000–6 and funding for the programme came principally from the Exchequer. All LEADER groups are private companies and their work extends to activities such as rural tourism and supporting local manufacturing. The board of each LEADER group comprises representatives from local authorities, state agencies, social partners and local communities. Post-2006, the work of LEADER groups is increasingly aligned with that of partnership companies and will play an important role in the development of the Rural Development Programme 2007–13.

---

[41] Irish Farm Holidays, Irish Country Holidays and Muintir na Tíre.

Vocational education committees

Turning from enterprise and development to education, there are 33 vocational educational committees (VECs) in the state, which by and large operate in areas congruent with local authority boundaries. VECs were established as corporate bodies under the Vocational Education Acts, 1930 to 2001, and their management is under the supervision of the Department of Education and Science rather than local authorities. However, a majority of the members of each VEC are elected members of local authorities, and under the most recent (2001) Act, certain functions are reserved for them.

The original purpose of VECs was to respond to local educational needs. By 'vocational', the 1930 Act referred to both continuation in education and technical (as opposed to academic) education. Their principal role has traditionally been the provision, administration and management of vocational schools and community colleges. Teaching staff in these institutions are employed by the VEC. Today VECs are involved not only in secondary education but also in post-secondary, further education and back-to-education programmes (see Chapter 8). The Vocational Education (Amendment) Act, 2001 reformed the financial, management and accountability structures in order to better achieve local requirements.[42]

City and county childcare committees

There are 33 childcare committees, operating in each county and city council area.[43] They were established as companies in 2001 to help provide and co-ordinate quality childcare services. They operate as working groups of the city and county development boards (below) and are represented on them, and at national level they are under the aegis of the Office of the Minister for Children. The boards of management of childcare committees comprise representatives of local and regional state organisations, the social partners, parents, childcare providers and voluntary organisations involved with childcare.

City and county development boards

The creation of a multitude of new bodies involved in enterprise and development at the local level raised issues concerning duplication and

---

[42] Curry, J. (2005) *Irish Social Services* (4th ed.). Dublin: Institute of Public Administration, p. 90.
[43] Galway County and City Councils share one such committee.

overlap with local authority work. In 1998, the *Report of the Task Force on the Integration of Local Government and Local Development Systems* recommended closer links between local authorities and local development bodies such as LEADER groups, enterprise boards and partnerships. This led to the establishment in 2000 of city and county development boards (CDBs) in every county and city council area. The principal role of the CDB is to ensure co-ordinated and coherent service delivery between all organisations operating locally, and they have a particular commitment to tacking social exclusion and promoting local development. CDBs are normally serviced by the local authority's community and enterprise section.

CDB board membership includes representatives of local authorities (both elected and administrative), national bodies (such as An Garda Síochána, Enterprise Ireland and FÁS), the social partners, local development bodies (such as LEADER groups, enterprise boards and childcare committees) and various other local non-governmental organisations and charities. In 2002, every CDB adopted a 10-year strategy for 'economic, social and cultural development' in the local authority area, and when planning their own work, all local organisations represented on the CDB must be cognisant of this strategy. CDBs are recognised as key mechanisms under the National Development Plan 2007–13 and the National Action Plan for Social Inclusion 2007–16.

As well as those bodies operating at local level, there are those that also operate on a larger regional basis. These regional bodies are involved in issues ranging from regional administration to fishing.

Regional authorities

Ireland does not have a system of democratically elected regional government. While the state is popularly divided into four provinces – Munster, Leinster, Ulster and Connacht – these have never been used for government or administrative purposes, apart from sport.[44] However, for the administration of EU funding, new administrative regions were created in 1994 and again in 1999 (Figure 12.3).

Under secondary legislation passed in 1993, eight regional authorities were established. The main roles of these authorities are to promote the co-ordination of public service provision and to monitor

---

[44] With the exception of Dublin, the provinces also form the constituency boundaries for European Parliament elections.

Figure 12.3. *Regional authorities (Source: Irish Regions Office website – www.iro.ie)*

the delivery of EU Structural Fund assistance in their respective regions. They do not have executive functions and do not provide services directly to the public. Each authority consists of elected members appointed from a number of local authorities, as follows.

- Border: Cavan, Donegal, Leitrim, Louth, Monaghan and Sligo
- Dublin: Dublin City, Dún Laoghaire-Rathdown, Fingal and South Dublin
- Mid-East: Kildare, Meath and Wicklow
- Midlands: Laois, Longford, Offaly and Westmeath
- Mid-West: Clare, Limerick City, Limerick County and North Tipperary

- South-East: Carlow, Kilkenny, South Tipperary, Waterford City, Waterford County and Wexford
- South-West: Cork City, Cork County and Kerry
- West: Galway City, Galway County, Mayo and Roscommon

The work of the authorities covers areas such as planning, development, environment and equality, and each has a director and a number of staff. The authorities review the development plans of local authorities in their region and prepare regional planning guidelines and economic and social strategies. As well as its work with local authority plans, each authority also has an EU operational committee. This committee assists the authority in relation to EU funding and reviews the implementation of various EU operational programmes in a region.

Regional assemblies

Ireland's receipt of EU funding has been instrumental in the establishment of another level of regional administration. Prior to 1999, Ireland was considered to be a single region for EU Structural Funds on the basis that the country as a whole was below the threshold to qualify for this funding. However, prosperity in the east and south of the country meant that the EU was unwilling to continue full funding (Objective 1 in EU terms) for these areas. The country was thus divided in two (according to regional authority boundaries), with a regional assembly for each region (Figure 12.4).

The Border, Midlands and Western (BMW) Regional Assembly consists of 29 elected members appointed from 13 local authorities – Cavan, Donegal, Galway, Laois, Leitrim, Longford, Louth, Mayo, Monaghan, Offaly, Roscommon, Sligo and Westmeath. The BMW Region achieved Objective 1 status for Structural Funds for the period 2000–6.

The Southern and Eastern (S&E) Regional Assembly consists of 41 elected members from the local authorities of Dublin City, Dun Laoghaire-Rathdown, Fingal, South Dublin, Carlow, Tipperary South, Waterford City, Wexford, Kilkenny, Cork City and County, Kerry, Clare, Limerick City and County, Tipperary North, Kildare, Meath and Wicklow. The S&E Region achieved Objective 1 (in transition) status for the period 2000–6.

The main duties of the assemblies are to manage funding programmes for their region under the National Development Plans and EU schemes, and to help co-ordinate and promote awareness of services within their regions. Each assembly has a director and a number of full-time staff.

Figure 12.4. *Areas corresponding to regional assemblies (Source: Irish Regions Office website – www.iro.ie)*

Regional fisheries boards

Under the 1980 Fisheries Act (and subsequent amendments), seven regional fisheries boards have responsibility for the conservation, protection, development, management and promotion of the state's inland fisheries. As well as a board, each has a chief executive and a small number of staff. The work of the boards is co-ordinated and supported by the Central Fisheries Board, an agency that advises the Minister for Communications, Energy and Natural Resources. Reform of the governance and functions of the boards has been advocated for a number of years, but at the time of writing no substantial changes had occurred.

13

The health services

The World Health Organisation defines health as 'a state of complete physical, mental and social well-being and not merely the absence or disease or infirmity'. In terms of personnel (over 100,000 employed directly and indirectly) and current expenditure (over €16 billion or 29% of overall current spending in Budget 2008), health is one of the largest sectors of the Irish public service. In this chapter, the principal national structures and reforms are examined, as are some of the state agencies involved in health and health-related services. While it is not possible to consider all aspects of the service, particular attention is given to the role of the Health Service Executive (HSE), which currently has operational control of the delivery of mainstream health and personal social services.

The administration of health services

While the extensive involvement of modern states in the provision of health services is a comparatively recent phenomenon, health services have by necessity traditionally been delivered through a complex network of administrative structures. Before considering recent reforms, it is necessary to sketch briefly the historical development of the Irish health services.[45]

The 1838 Poor Law (Ireland) Act represented the first state provision of health services, with the public workhouse system providing some elementary medical assistance. Subsequent legislation in the nineteenth century saw local authorities assume greater involvement in public health matters, and a Department of Local Government and Public Health was established in 1924. The focus of health care was mainly

---

[45] For more on this see Hensey, B. (1988) *The Health Services of Ireland.* Dublin: Institute of Public Administration; Curry, J. (2003) *Irish Social Services* (4th ed.). Dublin: Institute of Public Administration, Chapter 5; Wren, M.-A. (2003) *Unhealthy State: Anatomy of a Sick Society.* Dublin: New Island.

concerned with sanitation and infectious diseases such as tuberculosis, and hospitals remained a last resort for those in poverty.

From independence until the 1970 Health Act, health services were provided locally with relatively weak central co-ordination and modest financial assistance. Local authorities were charged with providing public health assistance and were also sanitary authorities with functions in respect of public health, and the Health Act of 1947 formally made the county and city (then known as county borough) councils health authorities for their areas. That year also saw a separate Department of Health being established, and a greater focus on women and children's health emerged.

As public hospital services were not guaranteed for all, demands for health insurance and the availability of private care emerged among those on higher incomes. This resulted in the establishment of a state enterprise called the Voluntary Health Insurance (VHI) Board under the Voluntary Health Insurance Act, 1957. Membership far exceeded the expected 15% of the population, and it was not until the 1990s that other private health insurance organisations emerged to challenge VHI's monopoly (see below).

In 1960, the city and county councils of Dublin, Cork, Limerick and Waterford respectively became joint authorities for health services, and a government White Paper on health services published in 1966 established the need for even greater fusion of existing services. In 1968, the (Professor Patrick) Fitzgerald report made several far-reaching recommendations, including:

- the need for centralisation of hospital services in a smaller number of larger, more specialised hospitals
- the establishment of an advisory body, Comhairle na nOspideal
- the need for the establishment of regional structures to oversee hospital services
- the need for planning and co-ordination in the provision of high-quality hospital care, particularly between the statutory and public voluntary hospital services
- the need to co-ordinate general practitioner and hospital care.

Further consolidation of health services came with the 1970 Health Act which established eight regional health boards covering the state. Also, health services were re-categorised under three programmes: Community Care, Special Hospital Care and General Hospital Care.

While local authorities were charged with appointing elected members to these new boards,[46] the Act effectively removed from local authorities any responsibility for substantive health service provision. This centralisation of health services during the twentieth century paralleled the shift in their funding from being largely a local matter to one funded by the Exchequer (see below).

During the 1980s, greater emphasis began to be placed on preventive measures, including health promotion and lifestyle issues. A consultation document in 1986 titled *Health – The Wider Dimensions* encouraged a more public-service-wide approach to health issues. It emphasised the impact of other sectors – agriculture, food, environment, housing, road safety, etc. – on the population's state of health. The need to establish a strategic framework for the health services culminated in the publication of the 1994 health strategy, *Shaping a Healthier Future*. The strategy sought to set targets for the achievement of public health objectives through greater integration of all service providers, particularly in the Dublin area. The traditional emphasis on caring and curing was accompanied by a much stronger focus on health promotion and illness prevention. The strategy was formulated around principles of equity, service quality and accountability. A major new departure for the health services was the explicit focus on the concepts of *health gain* and *social gain*. It was argued that only expenditure on health care that clearly added to health gain or social gain of the population should be accepted.

As a result of *Shaping a Healthier Future*, several institutional developments occurred, including the establishment of an Office for Health Gain, as well as the Eastern Regional Health Authority (ERHA), which replaced the Eastern Health Board and oversaw the work of three new area health boards for the densely populated eastern part of the country. It also resulted in the formation of the Health Boards Executive (HBE), an agency that acted on behalf of all health boards. Subsequent sectoral strategies emerged, including a National Strategy for Cancer Services in Ireland (1996), the Cardiovascular Health Strategy (1999), the National Health Promotion Strategy: 2000–2005 and the National Children's Strategy (2000).

In 2001, a new national health strategy was launched, titled *Quality and Fairness: A Health System For You*, which espoused similar

---

[46] The remainder of the board members were ministerial appointees or drawn from medical, nursing, dental and pharmaceutical professions.

principles to the 1994 strategy but with the addition of people-centredness. It focused on specific areas including:

- reform of the acute hospital system (including additional beds)
- strengthening primary care
- funding (its publication coincided with that of a consultancy report on value for money in the health system)
- human resources
- organisational reform
- information systems.

Following the 2001 strategy, a number of reports were commissioned considering different aspects of the increasingly large and expensive health service. These included the following.

- The *Audit of Structures and Functions in the Health System* (the Prospectus Report, 2003) concluded, *inter alia*, that there were too many health agencies and that the system lacked coherence at national and local levels for both planning and provision of services. It also called for better planning processes, needs assessments and stakeholder participation. The report recommended the abolition of the health boards and their replacement by a single unified body to fund the health system, the Health Service Executive. It also endorsed the establishment of an independent Health Information and Quality Authority (HIQA) to monitor the quality of services, a proposal first mooted in the Health Strategy (2001).
- The *Commission on Financial Management and Control Systems in the Health Services* (the Brennan Report, 2003) criticised the corporate governance arrangements within the system, including weak evaluation and information systems. It called for greater devolution of accountability to clinical consultants and GPs.
- The work of the *National Task Force on Medical Staffing* (the Hanly Report, 2003) included reviewing the average working time of non-consultant hospital doctors (NCHDs) and medical education and training needs as a consequence of the European Working Time Directive. Most prominently, it recommended significant reorganisation of acute hospital services, with larger hospitals concentrating on complex work and a greater development of day services in smaller hospitals.

Combined, these reports formed part of a new health reform programme that sought to separate policy from operation and that included the interim establishment of a new single entity – the Health Service Executive, as provided for in the Health Act, 2004.

The Health Service Executive
The Health Service Executive replaced the seven health boards, three area health boards and the ERHA. It began its work proper on 1 January 2005, and as of June 2007 had assumed the functions of 23 pre-existing agencies or boards working within the health sector. It is funded directly from the Exchequer under a vote separate to that of the Department of Health and Children, and the CEO of the HSE, rather than the minister, is an Accounting Officer in relation to that vote. The board of the HSE is appointed by the Minister for Health and Children. Its remit across health and social care is extensive, ranging from hospitals to community-based services and social services. Reflecting the atypical nature of the Irish health system, the HSE's remit also includes personal social services such as disability and children's and older people's services. Almost 70,000 staff are directly employed by the HSE and another 35,000 are funded by it.

The work of the HSE is overseen by an executive, which, according to the Health Act, 2004, has a duty to 'use the resources available to it in the most beneficial, effective and efficient manner to improve, promote and protect the health and welfare of the public' (Part 2, Section 7).

There are three principal divisions to the HSE, as follows.

- *Primary and Community and Continuing Care (PCCC).* This section is concerned with shifting the focus of health care away from hospitals to more local and community-based provision, and in particular services by general practitioners (GPs), public health nurses and other community-based health professionals. To assist in this process, hundreds of interdisciplinary primary care teams are being established nationwide and the National Development Plan 2007–13 has set a target of 500 such teams by 2011 (including the reconfiguration of existing services). The work of PCCC is delivered through 32 Local Health Offices who liaise as appropriate with the hospitals in their area.
- *Population Health.* The work of this section is concerned with the health of the population as a whole (including immunisations and

infectious diseases) and addressing inequalities between regions and groups.

- *National Hospitals Office.* This office co-ordinates the planning and provision of services by acute hospitals, as well as the ambulance services.

As Figure 13.1 illustrates, the work of these three divisions is administered according to four regional structures:

- Dublin North East
- West
- South
- Dublin Mid Leinster.

Within each of the four HSE areas is a regional health office. Also, each area has a regional health forum, which comprises local authority members and makes representations to the HSE on matters of relevance to its area. As well as the three divisions identified above, the work of the HSE is faciliated by its HR, finance, corporate planning, ICT and other offices.

Within its executive structure the HSE has a number of 'expert advisory groups' that allow for officials, clinical experts, service users and others to monitor and provide advice to the HSE on specific health areas such as cancer, mental health, disability and children.

Health Information and Quality Authority (HIQA)

The Health Information and Quality Authority (HIQA) was established in 2007 to 'drive quality, safety, accountability and the best use of resources in … health and social care services, whether delivered by public, voluntary or private bodies'. HIQA is charged with the independent oversight of health services to ensure quality and the provision of information on health services. HIQA also assumed the functions of the Social Services Inspectorate and the Irish Health Services Accreditation Board, and will be responsible for the independent inspection of facilities such as nursing homes and residential services for people with a disability.

It is the first agency of its kind in the Irish health system and is intended to take an independent, objective role, which includes analysing and commenting on particular aspects of the service, either on its own initiative or at the request of the minister. HIQA also has functions in relation to the co-ordination of health information and the development of health technology assessment.

Figure 13.1. *HSE regional structures (Source: An Introduction to the HSE (2007). Dublin: Health Services Executive)*

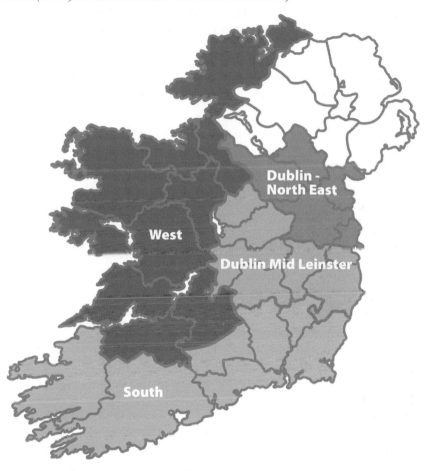

The Department of Health and Children

In an excellent example of how the role of the state has changed over the past 80 years, health did not feature as a separate ministerial portfolio upon the establishment of the Irish Free State. Instead, health functions were given to the Department of Local Government and Public Health and, as noted above, it was not until 1947 that a dedicated Department of Health was established (as well as a new Department of Social Welfare). However, the size and duties of the department were still relatively small compared to today, and up to the mid-1980s it was common for Ministers for Health to have responsibility for a second portfolio. In 1997 the department was renamed the Department of Health and Children.

The Department of Health and Children states that its role is to 'To improve the health and well-being of people in Ireland' by:

- supporting the delivery of high-quality, equitable and efficient health and personal social services
- leading change in the health system
- putting health at the centre of public policy
- promoting a 'whole of government' approach to health and social gain.

In other words, the department is responsible for the formulation and evaluation of overall health policy, and must work with the HSE to ensure delivery of the best possible health and social services. While the HSE is responsible for operational issues (and submits service and capital investment plans to the minister), the department sets the overall policy framework and the HSE must, for example, receive approval for its corporate plan from the minister. Also, the department must support its minister in the performance of his or her duties.

Compared with the HSE, the department is relatively small, with approximately 490 people employed in it. However, the range of policy areas is extensive, as evidenced by the divisions within the department and the matters they deal with, as follows.

- *Acute Hospitals and Associated Services*: Acute hospitals, blood policy, cancer policy
- *Continuing Care Policy*: Disability, long stay charges, mental health, services for older people
- *Eligibility and Public Health*: Eligibility, food and medicines, public health, public–private issues, health insurance unit
- *Finance, Information and Policy Support*: External ICT, finance, information, policy support, research/EU/international
- *National HR and Workforce Planning*: Health reform, medical and dental, nursing, professional/management and support, therapy advisory unit
- *Parliamentary and Corporate Affairs*: Change management, corporate services, general register office, HR, records management, legal affairs, legislation, press office
- *Primary Care and Social Inclusion*: Health promotion policy, primary care, food and medicines, public health, social inclusion

- *Office of the Minister for Children*: Co-ordination of all planning and services relating to children across government departments and agencies
- *Office for Disability and Mental Health*: Co-ordination of all planning and services relating to disability and mental health across government departments and agencies
- *Office for Older People*: Co-ordination of all planning and services relating to older people across government departments and agencies

The department also has a number of agencies under its remit, such as the Adoption Board, the Health Research Board, the Mental Health Commission and the National Cancer Forum. A particular feature of recent developments has been the establishment of offices to co-ordinate key activities of public agencies across government departments and other bodies. The Office of the Minister for Children was established in 2005 and the Offices for Older People and Disability and Mental Health in 2008. All three are headed by a separate minister of state.

In 2006, approximately €12 billion was spent on running the various health services, as shown in Table 13.1.[47]

Table 13.1. *Spending on health services, 2006*

Programme	€m
Community Protection	395
Community Health Services	2,399
Community Welfare	999
Mental Health	825
Disability	1,517
General Hospital	5,429
General Support	524
Total	12,088

As well as national commitments, the department is responsible for Ireland's health-related commitments to international organisations. As a member of the Organisation for Economic Co-operation and

[47] Department of Health and Children (2007) *Health in Ireland: Key Trends.* Dublin: Department of Health and Children.

Development, the United Nations, the European Union and the World Health Organisation (see Chapter 20), Ireland must fulfil certain duties including regular reporting of health statistics. In addition, involvement with these organisations allows Ireland input into agreed approaches to international health issues. Along with his or her counterparts, the minister is a member of the EU Health Council.

The hospital system

The contemporary Irish hospital network comprises public, voluntary and private hospitals. About half of our public hospital beds are provided in hospitals owned and operated by the HSE. The other half are provided by 'voluntary' hospitals which, though not owned by the state, are almost totally funded from public resources. Voluntary hospitals are effectively an integral part of the public hospital system. Private hospitals are operated on either a for-profit or not-for-profit basis, depending on their ownership, and account for about 12% of total acute hospital beds (public and private).

Many existing hospitals emerged in the eighteenth century as contributions by individuals and religious orders to public welfare. In addition to these 'voluntary' hospitals, state-funded hospitals and infirmaries were established by local authorities in the nineteenth century in the aftermath of the famine years; the mentally ill were placed in lunatic asylums. The twentieth century witnessed greater state involvement in the provision of health services, though this often caused tensions with existing providers and with the medical profession.[48] Many of today's specialist hospitals, which deal with issues such as cancer and infectious diseases, began their life as voluntary hospitals.

As the voluntary hospitals found it increasingly difficult to fund their services, a Hospitals Trust Fund was established in the 1930s. It was through this fund that a large portion of the proceeds from a state-run horse racing sweepstake was channelled until the 1980s, when the sweepstake ended. The trust fund formally ceased to exist with the establishment of the Health Service Executive (see below), but had ceased to be a significant source of funding many years before this. Service cutbacks in the 1980s led to a dramatic reduction in the number of public beds available in the hospital network. With the

---

[48] Curry, J. (2005) *Irish Social Services* (4th ed.). Dublin: IPA, pp. 122–4.

recent economic boom, the demand for greater and enhanced services has led to unprecedented increases in spending on hospitals and healthcare.

Privately owned hospitals are a small but important element of the Irish acute hospital system. Traditionally, government policy has been to work with them, largely as an add-on to the public system, and particularly as a provider of elective (non-emergency) surgery in selected specialties. In 2005 the government announced a major initiative whereby private hospitals could 'co-locate' on the site of public hospitals, with a view to increasing total acute bed capacity by about 1,000. Implementation of this policy is now proceeding, with some eight sites at varying stages of development at the time of writing. It is intended that the extra private beds in the co-located units will free up a corresponding amount of additional capacity for public patients in the adjacent public hospitals.

The provision of hospital services in Ireland has often been characterised as inefficient, and reforms are often stymied by local political pressures. A number of reports (Fitzgerald, 1968; Hanly, 2003) suggested the reorganisation of hospital services around regional hospitals which would provide acute (i.e. certain surgical or medical) services that smaller local hospitals could not cover. The National Treatment Purchase Fund was established in 2002 for patients awaiting public services to be treated privately, including the cost of travelling abroad for procedures if necessary. The great majority of patients using the NTPF are treated in Ireland, mostly in private hospitals.

Given that health provision is spread across hundreds of health centres, nursing homes, community hospitals and psychiatric hospitals, there is not room to discuss each here. Instead, basic elements of the General Medical Services (GMS) are considered – the GP and medical card systems.

General medical services

The smallest unit of the health services is the GP or local doctor. The origins of the modern-day GP lie in the nineteenth-century dispensary system, which emerged due to the inadequacy of county infirmaries and fever hospitals. Dispensaries were established in certain (but not all) parts of the country in which the poor were attended to free of charge by doctors paid for by the local authority. However, doctors also provided services to the fee-paying public in their private surgeries, thus ensuring that a two-tier system existed at the local level. This system was abolished in 1972 and all persons entitled to a medical card could be treated by a doctor of their choice (normally within a seven-mile radius) rather than having to attend a dispensary. Today, though effectively self-employed, doctors are paid from public funds for their treatment of medical card holders. Under the GMS system, pharmacists are the main providers of medicines to patients who are prescribed them by GPs. Prescribed medicines are provided free of charge by the state for medical card holders. All other patients meet an initial sum per month for prescribed drugs and the balance is met by the state.

Medical cards

Medical cards are provided to those of limited means and cover the cost for them (and their spouse and children) of services including GP visits, prescribed medicines, and dental, optical and other services. Medical cards are provided to all residents of the state over 70 years of age regardless of income. A GP Visit Card was introduced in 2005, covering the full cost of visiting a GP but not the cost of drugs. GP visit card-holders have an income that does not qualify them for a medical card but is lower than that of the non-medical-card population.

Funding health services today

Reflecting the role of local authorities in their delivery, for many decades after independence, local taxation was a prominent source of revenue for the administration of health services. In the aftermath of the Second World War, the Exchequer still contributed less than a fifth of the total cost of services. From the 1950s onwards, the contribution from central government increased as a percentage of the total to a point where, by the mid-1970s, local funding was no longer deemed appropriate. The decision to remove health charges from local rates coincided with the transfer of the burden of paying domestic rates from homeowners to the state. Thus from this period onwards, funding the health services has been a concern of the Department of Health.

The dire economic straits of the 1980s resulted in swingeing cuts to the health sector, and the 'Celtic Tiger' years witnessed increasingly large portions of the social services budget being channelled into health in order to compensate for this earlier chronic under-funding. In 1989 a Commission on Health Funding produced a report that went beyond immediate financial issues and commented on the need for better planning and organisation in the delivery of services in order to achieve better value for money.

By far the greatest part of funding for public health services comes from the Exchequer by way of general taxation (82%) and a separate health levy (9%). The balance of public funding comes from charges (A&E and charges for private/semi-private care in public hospitals) and under EU Regulations (in respect of residents from other EU countries).

Health insurance
By the 1950s, access to hospital services was income-based and three levels of eligibility applied. Those in the lowest income cohort had access to free hospital treatment, middle-income groups had entitlement to free or subsidised public hospital treatment, and the top income cohort (15%) had no entitlement to hospital services. A demand for health insurance emerged from the last of these cohorts. The report of an advisory board established in 1956 led to the establishment of the Voluntary Health Insurance (VHI) Board under the Voluntary Health Insurance Act, 1957. The board is under the aegis of the Minister for Health and Children and is a non-profit enterprise; any surpluses are expected to benefit policy-holders.

While original expectations were that membership of VHI would not exceed the proportion of the population that was not entitled to public hospital services, the demand for private and semi-private hospital services led to exponential growth in membership. By 2007 VHI had over 1.5 million members and 75% of the total health insurance market. The monopoly of the VHI had ended with the entry of the British United Provident Association (BUPA) to the market in 1997 as a result of its liberalisation under the 1994 Health Insurance Act.

A third provider, VIVAS, entered the market in 2003, and when BUPA withdrew from the Irish market in 2006 its assets were purchased by another Irish provider, Quinn Insurance. The Health Insurance Authority has regulated the market since 2001. In spite of a phased extension of eligibility for public hospital services (from 1979 the top 15% of income earners were covered for services in public hospitals, other than meeting consultant fees, and in 1991 they became eligible for public consultant services also), it is striking that the demand for health insurance has continued to grow. Today, just over half of the Irish adult population has private health insurance.

The public–private debate

As described above, healthcare in Ireland has not always been the sole preserve of the state, and many of the largest hospitals are owned and run by religious orders. In addition, the voluntary sector plays a substantial role in a number of social services such as those for people with a disability and services for older people. However, it is private provision of hospital services that generates much debate, particularly because many of these private services are subsidised by public funds. While those on the lowest income thresholds have access to free primary care, most Irish adults must pay towards the cost of treatment, either through health insurance (which is limited in the primary care sector) or out of their own resources.

That many of the services covered by private health insurance schemes are delivered in public hospital facilities has been a consistent source of public discussion, and is one of the more explicit manifestations of Ireland's unusual mix of public, private and voluntary involvement in the provision of health services. Also, the introduction of tax breaks for privately owned hospitals in 2001 and the subsequent decision to allow private hospitals to be built on public lands (the co-location initiative discussed above) have generated considerable discussion concerning the equity of health services.

Similarly, the agreement on a 'common contract' for medical consultants in 1979 has received considerable attention in recent years. It has been subject to a number of reviews since then, most recently in 2007–8. The original contract arose as an attempt to consolidate differing conditions of employment for consultants in voluntary and health board hospitals. The former depended on private practice for their income while the latter received a state salary and had some opportunity for private practice. The new contract required all consultants to work for 33 hours a week in public hospitals for a public salary, but allowed private practice, much of which could be performed using public facilities.

Today, consultants receive a salary in respect of their public patients (in a 33-hour week) and, depending the conditions of their contract, can practise privately on the site of their main public commitment and/or off-site. With over 2000 consultants now working in the health services, and greater than ever demand for specialist consultancy services, the appropriate relationship between the state and consultants continues to be a source of much debate.

Other health services

Before leaving this chapter, it should be noted that strategies for reform of the mental health care and disability services have been launched in recent years. Recognising that considerable numbers of the population suffer from either mental health problems (*A Vision for Change*, 2006) or a disability (*National Disability Strategy*, 2004 and *Sectoral Plans in Six Government Departments*, 2006), the plans provide considerable financial resources and a move towards more specialist and tailored services for patients.

Professionals with the health services

The activities of a number of professions within the health services have been regulated by a number of agencies, some of which are established by those professions but carry out this important public function. For example, doctors are regulated by the Medical Council, nurses by An Bord Altranais and pharmacists by the Pharmaceutical Society of Ireland. In 2005 the Health and Social Care Professionals Act provided for the establishment of an additional number of registration boards covering the following 12 professions:

- clinical biochemists
- psychologists
- chiropodists/podiatrists
- dieticians
- orthoptists
- physiotherapists
- radiographers
- speech and language therapists
- occupational therapists
- social workers
- medical scientists
- social care workers and resident managers.

In conclusion, the size and nature of the health services ensure that they remain a key element of public expenditure and hence state involvement. As detailed above, recent years have witnessed significant developments in rationalising a system that has emerged from a variety of sources and in an irregular manner in order to achieve greater public outcomes and improvements in general population health. Maintaining and building on this progress will continue to require considerable political and administrative commitment.

14

The education system

The modern state is expected to provide its citizens with ever-greater levels of education. In the Republic of Ireland, it is compulsory for all children between the ages of six and 16 to attend full-time education. The Budget for 2008 earmarked €9.3 billion for the Department of Education – approximately 16% of total funds. The development of the education system reflects that of the health system in terms of its mix of public, church and voluntary interests and the periodic emergence of tensions between these stakeholders. While state-funded pre-primary schooling schemes are increasingly common, in this chapter the emergence and current structures of the education system at primary, secondary, further and third levels are considered.

Unlike many other aspects of state activity, the 1937 Constitution contains several provisions relating to education.[49] They are worth repeating here (Table 14.1).

Primary education

While the first state structure designed to address the issue of primary education was the 1831 National Board of Education, the education of children had been a core feature of various religious denominations prior to this. The board was instrumental in the establishment of denominational (mainly Catholic but also Church of Ireland) teacher training institutions during the latter half of the nineteenth century, and provided grants for the building of schools. The Irish Education Acts of 1892 and 1898 provided for primary education for those between the ages of six and 14, and the numbers of children receiving such elementary education increased rapidly in the early years of the twentieth century. With the establishment of the Department of Education in 1922, the board ceased to exist. The department inherited

---

[49] Coolahan also refers to this (Coolahan, J. (1981) *Irish Education: History and Structure*. Dublin: Institute of Public Administration, p. 155).

Table 14.1. *Articles of the Constitution relating to education*

Article 42

1.   The State acknowledges that the primary and natural educator of the child is the Family and guarantees to respect the inalienable right and duty of parents to provide, according to their means, for the religious and moral, intellectual, physical and social education of their children.
2.   Parents shall be free to provide this education in their homes or in private schools or in schools recognised or established by the State.
3.1 The State shall not oblige parents in violation of their conscience and lawful preference to send their children to schools established by the State, or to any particular type of school designated by the State.
3.2 The State shall, however, as guardian of the common good, require in view of actual conditions that the children receive a certain minimum education, moral, intellectual and social.
4.   The State shall provide for free primary education and shall endeavour to supplement and give reasonable aid to private and corporate educational initiative, and, when the public good requires it, provide other educational facilities or institutions with due regard, however, for the rights of parents, especially in the matter of religious and moral formation.
5.   In exceptional cases, where the parents for physical or moral reasons fail in their duty towards their children, the State as guardian of the common good, by appropriate means shall endeavour to supply the place of the parents, but always with due regard for the natural and imprescriptible rights of the child.

Article 44

2.4 Legislation providing State aid for schools shall not discriminate between schools under the management of different religious denominations, nor be such as to affect prejudicially the right of any child to attend a school receiving public money without attending religious instruction at that school.
2.6 The property of any religious denomination or any educational institution shall not be diverted save for necessary works of public utility and on payment of compensation.

---

a system of primary schools that were overwhelmingly denominational; as of 2007 over 90% of primary schools had as their patrons the Catholic Church. The state's continued support of free primary education is enshrined in Article 42.4 of the Constitution (Table 14.1).

While the Catholic Church-owned and parish-based 'national' schools are the most common, a small number are run by other faiths or by non-faith organisations. All are subsidised by the state, although a few non-subsidised fee-paying private schools also exist. There are several state-funded Gaelscoileanna in which educational instruction is delivered through the Irish language, while some other Gaelscoileanna are funded by a limited company – Foras Pátrúnachta na Scoileanna LánGhaeilge. It is only since 1999 that the state has insisted on retaining ownership of school buildings that it pays for, as opposed to their retention by the patrons. Since the mid-1970s, most primary schools have been managed by a board of management consisting of representatives of the patron, the Department of Education, parents and teachers. The boards are elected for three years at a time, are responsible for such issues as the appointment and removal of teachers, and have a chairperson nominated by the patron. In the 2006/7 academic year, over 470,000 students passed through the primary school system, taught by approximately 28,700 teachers. The Department of Education and Science sets and monitors the primary curriculum. It also pays teachers' salaries, determines the terms and conditions of their employment and evaluates their work.

Second-level education

Second-level education in Ireland is delivered through four types of school – secondary, vocational, comprehensive and community (Table 14.2).

Table 14.2. *Numbers of second-level schools and students*[50]

Type of school	Number of students 2006/7	Number of schools	Number of teachers, June 2007
Secondary	183,721	394	27,363
Vocational	97,681	247	
Comprehensive and Community	52,316	91	
Total	333,718	732	

[50] Data from Department of Education and Science and Central Statistics Offices websites accessed November 2007, and personal communication with Department of Education and Science.

Secondary schools

The most common type of post-primary school in Ireland is the secondary school. The Intermediate Education Act of 1878 provided funding to support those moving from primary to higher education, including their progress through a series of examinations. As with primary education, the functions of the Intermediate Education Board established under the Act were assumed by the new Department of Education on Independence, and a new system of intermediate and leaving certificates was introduced. Funding was provided according to the number of pupils in each school, although a different scheme was devised for Protestant schools involving the distribution of funds to parents rather than schools. Also, secondary schools tended to be single-sex. Despite state funding, access to many voluntary second-level educational institutions was still dependent on payment of fees, and kept such education out of reach for a large portion of society up to 1967.

A landmark publication in the widening of access to second-level education was the *Investment in Education* report of 1965, commissioned by then minister and later President Patrick Hillery. It drew attention to the unequal access to post-primary schools due to geography and socio-economic status. It was in response to this publication that Hillery's successor as minister, Donogh O'Malley, introduced free access to secondary education and later free transport to and from school for pupils living more than three miles away. However, unlike the situation in other states, provision was not made for universal free school meals or medical services for students; instead, grants were made available towards the costs of books and other items. The numbers attending secondary school rose dramatically following the introduction of these new schemes.

Today, all secondary schools receive public funding but remain privately owned and managed. In most cases the trustees are the religious communities or boards of governors. The intermediate examination is now called the Junior Certificate and is taken after three years, while Leaving Certificate exams (including Leaving Certificate Applied) are normally taken two or three (including a transition year) years after the Junior Cert, when students are 17 or 18 years of age.

Vocational schools

While the majority of students received academic education, an acknowledgement that education of students in technical skills was desirable led to the establishment of the vocational education system by virtue of the Vocational Education Act, 1930, which created vocational education committees (VECs) throughout the state (principally along local authority contours). As noted in Chapter 12, VECs provide, administer and manage vocational schools and community colleges and are also involved in post-secondary further education and back-to-education programmes. The boards of management of vocational schools are sub-committees of the VEC area in which they are situated. While they did not originally offer Leaving Certificate qualifications, vocational schools have done so since the 1960s. Their principal goal is to provide education in response to local needs, and they had a tradition of being interdenominational. The Vocational Education (Amendment) Act, 2001 reformed the membership of the VECs, as well as their management and financial accountability.

Comprehensive and community schools

The *Investment in Education* report also led to the establishment of two further types of post-primary school – comprehensive and community.

Comprehensive schools were built in areas that previously had inadequate or no access to second-level education. They offered both academic and technical education and so were something a hybrid of the existing secondary and vocational schools. Significantly, they were completely financed by the Department of Education, and a number of Protestant comprehensives exist.

Community schools were the product of mergers between vocational and secondary schools in response to calls for greater rationalisation of resources in areas well served by access to second-level education. Community schools were to be non-denominational and, as the capital and current costs were to be almost completely paid by the state (the remainder by VECs and religious orders), did not require students to pay fees. The community and comprehensive schools are managed by boards of management of differing compositions including representatives of religious orders, parents and teachers.

Further education

Apart from third-level education (see below), there are a number of post-second-level education and training schemes that are collectively referred to as the 'further education' sector. The principal such schemes are as follows.

- *Post-Leaving Certificate (PLC) courses.* The PLC programme began in 1985 and offers full-time vocational training programmes. They include training in technical subjects such as IT and multimedia, cultural subjects such as performing arts and design, and other diverse areas including horticulture and equestrian studies. The focus of these courses is to enable students to make an easier transition to the workforce.
- *The Back to Education Initiative (BTEI).* This scheme is primarily aimed at young adults who seek opportunities to return to learning and develop new skills in order to improve employment opportunities.
- *The Vocational Training Opportunity Scheme (VTOS).* This scheme is open to unemployed people over 21 years of age, and lasts for two years. It is managed by the VECs (see Chapter 12) and covers a range of courses similar to those offered at Junior and Leaving Certificate levels for which certificates are awarded on completion.
- *The Adult Literacy Services Scheme.* These schemes are also run by the VECs and provide opportunities for adults with low literacy skills to improve on them. The National Adult Literacy Agency also contributes to the work of this scheme.

Third-level education

In 2006, almost a quarter of those aged 15–64 in Ireland had a third-level qualification. Irish third-level education is provided by both universities and non-university institutions. While the majority of third-level institutions are state-funded, a small but increasing number of private ones have emerged in recent years. College attendance is outlined in Table 14.3.

Table 14.3. *Numbers attending state-aided third-level colleges*[51]

Aided third-level colleges	Number of students 2006/7
HEA-funded universities	82,488
Teacher training	1,190
Institutes of technology/Technological colleges	52,887
Other (aided by Department of Education and Science)	1,797
Total	138,362

[51] Data provided in personal communication with Department of Education and Science.

Universities

There are seven university colleges in Ireland. The University of Dublin has one college, Trinity College, which was established by charter in 1592. The National University of Ireland was established by charter in 1908 and has four constituent colleges, in Dublin (Univerity College Dublin), Cork (University College Cork), Maynooth (National University of Ireland, Maynooth) and Galway (National University of Ireland, Galway). The final two universities are the University of Limerick and Dublin City University. The universities are principally concerned with undergraduate and postgraduate training and research.

Institutes of Technology/Technical Colleges

As well as introducing free access to second-level education, Donogh O'Malley is credited with bringing to fruition plans for the introduction of regional technical colleges (RTCs) in areas where there was no third-level institution in close proximity. Their management was originally within the remit of the local VEC. With the decline in agriculture and the growing industrial sector, RTCs were designed to provide post-secondary specialist training on a regional basis. The first RTCs opened in Athlone, Carlow, Dundalk, Sligo and Waterford in 1970 and were followed by others,[52] bringing the total to 13 by 2000.

Under the Regional Technical Colleges Act, 1992, the RTCs achieved greater independence, including the establishment of their own governing authorities. In 1997 the RTCs were renamed as Institutes of Technology. In addition to the 13 regional institutes, the Dublin Institute of Technology was established as an independent institution under the Dublin Institute of Technology Act, 1992. The Act brought together six colleges of higher education formerly under the City of Dublin VEC, namely:

- Kevin Street College of Technology
- Mountjoy Square College of Marketing and Design
- Chatham Row College of Music
- Rathmines College of Commerce
- Cathal Brugha Street College of Catering
- Bolton Street College of Technology.

---

[52] Letterkenny (1971), Galway-Mayo (1972), Cork (1974), Tralee (1977), Tallaght (1992), Limerick (1993), Dún Laoghaire (1997) and Blanchardstown (2000).

Today, approximately 40% of all students pursuing third-level qualifications do so through the technological colleges.

Colleges of education/Teacher training
Another type of third-level institution in Ireland is the colleges of education. They principally serve to provide training for primary teachers, as well as in certain disciplines for post-primary schools. They include the Mater Dei Institute of Education (Dublin), Mary Immaculate College (Limerick), St Patrick's College (Dublin) and St Angela's College (Sligo).

Other third-level institutions
Finally, the state provides varying levels of funding to a number of other third-level institutions, including the National College of Art and Design and the Tipperary Rural and Business Development Institute.

Agencies within the education sector

The Department of Education and Science has a number of agencies within its remit, including the following.

The Higher Education Authority (HEA)
The HEA has responsibility for planning and developing higher education and research in Ireland. It also has responsibility for the distribution of state funding within the third-level sector.

State Examinations Commission
This commission is charged with developing and overseeing second-level examinations, i.e. the Junior and Leaving Certificate exams. It was established in 2003 and assumed functions that had previously been performed within the Department of Education and Science.

National Education Welfare Board
The board was established in 2002 and is responsible for ensuring that all children in the state either attend a school or otherwise receive an education, including home-based education. It is also involved with issues of school attendance and educational welfare.

Higher Education and Training Awards Council (HETAC)
HETAC was established in 2001 and is the qualifications-awarding body for those third-level educational and training institutions that operate outside the university sector.

Finally, it should be noted that not all education services are solely within the remit of the Department of Education and Science. For example, the Department of Justice, Equality and Law Reform has responsibilities in relation to the education of young offenders, while the Department of Agriculture and Food funds training in agricultural issues.

15

Justice and the courts

Chapters 3 to 7 have considered the workings of two of the three pillars of state – the legislature that makes laws and the executive that implements them. In this chapter, the third or judicial pillar and its powers are considered. In essence, the judicial pillar is concerned with the meaning of law and the manner of its application. The chapter therefore considers the principal institutions involved in this role – the courts – as well as the state's various legal offices and officers.

The principal courts

Article 34.1 of the Constitution provides that:

> Justice shall be administered in courts established by law by judges appointed in the manner provided by this Constitution, and, save in such special and limited cases as may be prescribed by law, shall be administered in public.

The four principal courts in Ireland are the District Court, Circuit Court, High Court and Supreme Court (Figure 15.1). The Constitution (Article 34.3.4) refers to courts of 'local and limited' jurisdiction – these are the District and Circuit Courts. The state's superior courts are the High Court, Supreme Court and Court of Criminal Appeal. Each court has its own jurisdiction and powers. The administration of justice through the courts system is held in public except for some delicate matters (such as family law matters) which may be dealt with in camera.

The courts are presided over by judges, who are appointed by the President on the advice of the government. The government selects candidates for positions following a shortlisting process conducted by the Judicial Appointments Advisory Board. In order for justice to be conducted in an impartial manner, the judges of all courts must be free from financial or political pressures. On taking office, under Article 34.5.1 of the Constitution, judges pledge:

Figure 15.1. *Hierarchy of principal courts in Ireland*

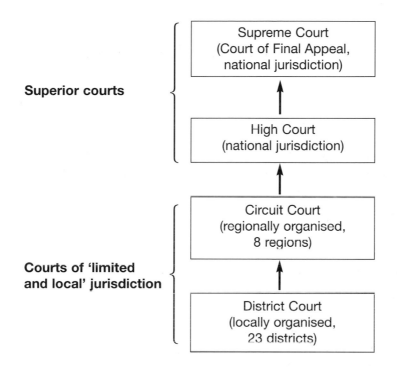

to duly and faithfully and to the best of my knowledge and power execute the office of [...] without fear or favour, affection or ill-will towards any man, and that I will uphold the Constitution and the laws.

The Constitution therefore provides that once appointed, judges shall hold office for life, except for their removal in certain extenuating circumstances, e.g. stated misbehaviour or incapacity, which can only occur by resolutions passed by both Houses of the Oireachtas. Also, their remuneration cannot be reduced while in office.

Before considering the jurisdictions of the various courts, an important distinction must be drawn between civil and criminal law matters. Criminal law is concerned with defining a range of actions prohibited by the state and the punishment of those who break these laws. Civil law, on the other hand, is largely concerned with the resolution of disputes between private individuals and includes such issues as personal injuries or breaches of contract.

District Court (An Chúirt Dúiche)

The District Court consists of the President of the District Court and 60 judges. From 2008, the country outside of the Dublin Metropolitan District area will be divided into 24 districts. The districts are further divided into over 150 District Court areas. Each district has a judge permanently assigned to it, with the exception of the Dublin Metropolitan District, which has a number of judges.

The President of the District Court is charged with the prompt and efficient discharge of business throughout the country. The District Court is a court of *summary jurisdiction*, in which a single judge sits without a jury. It is the most common type of court and deals with the greatest number of (relatively minor) cases. Decisions of the District Court can be appealed to the Circuit Court, with some exceptions. Examples of issues that fall within the remit of the District Court are as follows.

* In criminal law:
  – minor offences where there is no right of trial by jury
  – indictable offences (i.e. offences that may attract jury trial) where both the District Court judge and the Director of Public Prosecutions (DPP – see below) do not object (in some cases the accused may be asked to waive his or her right to jury trial also)
* In civil law:
  – The District Court can award damages up to €6,348.69.

The District Court also has functions in relation to licences (such as those for lotteries or the sale of alcohol) and some family law-related matters (such as care orders, domestic violence and the guardianship of children).

When dealing with children under 18 who are charged with criminal offences, the District Courts are known as Children Courts. In Dublin, a dedicated Children Court exists independently and sits on every working day.

The Circuit Court (An Chúirt Chuarda)

The Circuit Court consists of the President of the Court and 37 judges. The President of the Circuit Court is *ex officio* a member of the High Court. While the Circuit Court is one entity, for the purposes of its work the country is divided into eight circuits. A permanent judge is appointed in six of the country circuits, while Dublin has 10 permanent judges and Cork has three. The Circuit Court can sit in different venues within its circuit. It hears appeals from the District Court on both civil and criminal matters, and in regard to decisions of the Labour Court and the Employment Appeals Tribunal. There are also 26 Circuit Court offices throughout the country, each with a County Registrar in charge of its work.

- In criminal law:
  - with the exception of serious offences such as murder, rape or aggravated sexual assault, the Circuit Court can deal with most indictable offences. These are offences that may or must be heard by a judge and jury. In non-minor criminal matters the Constitution requires that the court comprise a judge and jury. When dealing with criminal matters, it sits as a Circuit Criminal Court.
- In civil law:
  - the Circuit Court can hear appeals on matters from the District Courts
  - it can award damages up to €38,092.14.

In terms of family law, the Circuit Court has wider jurisdiction than the District Court in relation to domestic violence and the guardianship of children. It also has the power to make decrees of divorce, judicial separation and nullity.

The High Court (An Ard-Chúirt)
The High Court consists of a President and 37 ordinary judges. They are joined by the President of the Circuit Court and the Chief Justice (see below) who act as *ex-officio* members. The High Court is normally based in the Four Courts in Dublin but can move location as need arises. The judgments of the High Court are capable of forming precedents that must be followed in the lower courts.

- In criminal law:
  - when exercising its jurisdiction in criminal law matters, the High Court is referred to as the *Central Criminal Court*. It hears the more serious cases such as murder and rape. As noted above, the Constitution requires non-minor matters to be heard by a judge and jury.
- In civil law:
  - the High Court is an appeal court for matters arising from the Circuit Court

- it can award unlimited damages and for many cases the judge can hear the case on his own. Juries normally apply to cases of defamation, assault or malicious prosecution.
- it can hear constitutional challenges to legislation brought by citizens
- it can review decisions made by tribunals (see below).

The High Court also supervises the work of the Circuit and District Courts.

The Supreme Court (An Chúirt Uachtarach)

The Supreme Court is the highest court in the state and the final court of appeal. On appeal from the High Court or on referral by the President, it determines the constitutional validity of law. Most of the cases it hears are appeal cases arising from lower courts, and particularly the Circuit Court. In 2006 it dealt with over 200 such appeals. It is housed in the Four Courts in Dublin and consists of the President of the court (the Chief Justice) and seven other judges. The President of the High Court is also *ex officio* an additional member of the Supreme Court. Not all members of the court are required to attend for the Supreme Court to perform its business, and it may hear more than one case at a time. For example, for appeals or cases that do not involve major legal matters, the court need only consist of three members; if an issue such as the constitutionality of a statute is challenged or if an important matter of law arises, the court consists of five judges. Only in exceptional circumstances, such as the referral of a Bill by the President (see Chapter 3), do seven judges sit.

Other courts

The Special Criminal Court

The Special Criminal Court was re-established in 1972, having originally been provided for in the Offences against the State Act, 1939, which introduced the concept of special courts at the start of the Second World War. It is used today for dealing with matters such as firearms offences or offences associated with organised crime. The court consists of three judges (one each from the High, District and Circuit Courts) appointed by the government and does not have a jury. An appeal against a sentence handed down by the Special Criminal Court may be taken to the Court of Criminal Appeal.

Court of Criminal Appeal

The Court of Criminal Appeal hears appeals arising from sentences and convictions by the Special Criminal Court, the Central Criminal Court (the criminal division of the High Court) or the Circuit Criminal Court. It also hears appeals from courts martial as well as sentences that are appealed by the Director of Public Prosecutions on the basis of 'undue leniency'. In exceptional circumstances, appeals from the Court of Criminal Appeal are heard by the Supreme Court. In 2006, over 300 appeals were disposed of in the Court of Criminal Appeal.

Figure 15.2. *Course of appeal in the Criminal Courts*

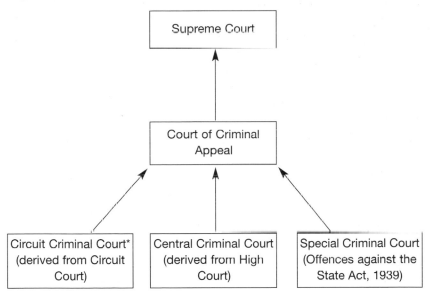

* For a case to be heard by the Supreme Court from the Court of Criminal Appeal, the Director of Public Prosecutions, the Attorney General or the Court of Criminal Appeal itself must certify that the point of law involved is one of exceptional public importance.

Commercial Court

In 2002, due to the growing number of cases relating to commercial law, a Committee on Court Practice and Procedure recommended the establishment of a Commercial Court in Dublin. It operates as a separate division within the High Court and thus reduced the burden of work within that court. It began its work in January 2004, and two judges alternate between cases.

The Courts Service

The Courts Service Act, 1998 provided for the establishment of an agency to oversee the management and administration of the courts. The agency – the Courts Service – came into being the following year and also provides support services for the judiciary. As well as its offices in Dublin, the service has five regional offices supporting the Circuit and District Courts. It oversees the renovation of the courts, many of which were in need of refurbishment after years of neglect.

The service is governed by a board consisting of a chairperson and 16 other members, and the senior management team comprises the Chief Executive Officer and seven directors. It is funded by the state through the Department of Justice, Equality and Law Reform. The CEO of the Courts Service is an Accounting Officer and therefore responsible for the use of the service's funds.

The legal profession

The legal profession in Ireland is divided into two branches, solicitors and barristers. The distinctions between these are still quite prominent. In almost all cases a person with a legal problem must first consult a solicitor for legal advice. A barrister is not permitted to take instructions directly from a member of the public in most cases. Broadly speaking, a solicitor tends to specialise in legal work that involves the preparation of cases for court rather than for advocacy in court. A barrister tends to specialise in the preparation of cases for court as well as advocacy itself. The barrister may only give legal advice after receiving instructions from a solicitor, a practice that has been criticised on competition grounds in recent years. Solicitors may form a partnership as a firm of solicitors, while barristers may only practise as sole traders. They do not practise together in chambers as in England. Also, unlike solicitors, barristers may not advertise themselves or their work.

Solicitors

In order to become a solicitor, a candidate must serve a period of apprenticeship with an established solicitor for a minimum of two years. He or she must also complete the courses of study organised by the Law Society at Blackhall Place. The prospective solicitor is expected to hold a university degree or its equivalent. The solicitor's profession is self-regulated, i.e. the Law Society controls issues of recruitment and standards within the profession, and solicitors must pay an annual fee to the Law Society to maintain their practice.

Solicitors can deal with a wide range of issues, from non-contentious matters such as drafting wills or conveyancing (transferring a legal title for a property from one person to another) to contentious personal injury cases. These issues do not normally involve the courts, although solicitors may represent their clients in the District Courts in relation to minor matters such as a road traffic offence. Although since the Courts Act of 1971 solicitors may appear in any court up to and including the Supreme Court, this rarely occurs outside the District Court.

Barristers

In order to become a barrister, candidates must pursue a barrister-at-law degree with the Honourable Society of King's Inns. Once qualified, a barrister is 'called to the Bar' in the Supreme Court. Barristers practise from the Law Library within the Four Courts. Once a barrister enters the Law Library, he or she must 'devil' or serve an apprenticeship for one year with an established barrister.

Barristers are divided into two categories according to seniority and expertise – junior counsel and senior counsel – with the majority being junior counsel. A senior counsel is a barrister who has applied for this rank and generally has significant experience and some areas of particular skill and expertise. He or she will normally appear in the higher courts more frequently than junior counsel.

The state's law officers

In the administration and pursuit of judicial matters, the state employs several specialist legal officers. Apart from the Office of the Attorney General (see Chapter 7), these include the Director of Public Prosecutions and the Chief State Solicitor.

The Director of Public Prosecutions

The Office of the Director of Public Prosecutions (DPP) was established in 1974, and assumed functions previously performed by the Attorney General. The role of the office is to prosecute all serious crimes in the name of the people, and the office often appears in court cases as *The State (DPP)*. The DPP is appointed by the government, and although part of the public service, he or she is independent and may initiate cases as is necessary.

Within the Office of the DPP, a Chief Prosecution Solicitor oversees the work of a number of solicitors who prepare cases on behalf of the DPP. Outside Dublin, the Chief Prosecution Solicitor is assisted by 32 local state solicitors who prepare cases on his or her behalf. The DPP's office also employs a number of barristers to prosecute cases on his behalf.

The Chief State Solicitor

As the state is involved with an ever-increasing amount of litigation, it is necessary for it to have a legal officer who can represent it and brief junior and senior counsel accordingly. This role is performed by the Chief State Solicitor, which is a constituent part of the Attorney General's office (see Chapter 7 for more on the Attorney General). The office-holder acts as solicitor to the Attorney General, government departments and other public organisations. Prior to 2002 when the function was transferred to the Office of the Chief Prosecution Solicitor (see above), the Chief State Solicitor's office acted as a solicitor to the DPP and provided and managed the local state solicitor service.

The Chief State Solicitor's office is divided into five legal divisions, namely advisory, justice and common law, asylum and legal services, public law and state property. Together these divisions manage a range of issues from conveyancing of state property to acting on behalf of the government before the European Court of Justice (ECJ), to supplying legal staff for tribunals of inquiry (see below).

Tribunals

While all criminal matters must be resolved in the courts, many civil and administrative matters can be settled by a tribunal. The power of tribunals is normally restricted and they do not involve a jury. Also, they are established by legislation that sets out the powers of the tribunal and the procedures that will be applied in the course of its work. There are two different types of tribunal: permanent or rights tribunals, and tribunals established to consider a specific matter after which they cease to exist (tribunals of inquiry). They may be held in public or in private.

Rights tribunals

A rights tribunal more closely resembles a court in its work. It makes binding decisions on disputes between parties. The legislation establishing the tribunal sets out how many members will sit on the tribunal and whether they will be lawyers, civil servants or representatives of particular sectors of the economy or society. It also sets out the powers of the tribunal and the procedures that will be applied. Such tribunals are established to provide a quick, informal and inexpensive alternative to the courts system in a specific area of law.

The decisions of most rights tribunals can be appealed to the courts. Parties appearing before a rights tribunal generally have to pay for their own legal representation.

Some of the better-known rights tribunals are as follows.

- *The Criminal Injuries Compensation Tribunal* decides the level of compensation to be paid to persons who have suffered injuries in the course of a criminal act.
- *The Employment Appeals Tribunal* hears and decides cases in which an employee claims he or she has been unfairly dismissed.
- *The Labour Court* investigates disputes between employers and employees and makes recommendations.
- *The Refugee Appeals Tribunal* hears appeals by asylum-seekers against decisions to refuse them refugee status.
- *An Bord Pleanála* hears appeals against either the granting or the refusing of planning permission by a planning authority.
- *The Valuation Tribunal* hears disputes in relation to the rateable valuation of properties. The rateable valuation is the value that the local authority puts on property for the purpose of deciding what rates (taxes) will be charged.

Tribunals of inquiry

A tribunal of inquiry has a different function; it is inquisitorial in nature rather than a forum for the administration of justice. It simply investigates a specific matter of urgent public importance and submits a report to the Oireachtas setting out its findings of fact. Prior to the 1990s, tribunals of inquiry investigated issues such as fire disasters and exporting matters; post-1990 they became associated with investigating issues of maladministration and corruption.

To carry out the investigation, the tribunal is given certain powers by the Oireachtas, including the power to hold public or private hearings. The Oireachtas may decide that any tribunal it establishes will be invested with the powers set out in the various Tribunals of Inquiry Acts that date back as far as 1921. Recent tribunals of inquiry have faced a variety of legal challenges and as a result the Oireachtas has had to pass several new Acts to facilitate their work.

Tribunals of inquiry can normally make orders to oblige witnesses to attend and give evidence, and can apply to the High Court if a person refuses to give evidence or is in contempt of the tribunal. Continued failure to comply can lead to imprisonment. Tribunals can also determine who should pay the costs of another person appearing before the tribunal, as well as the cost of the tribunal itself. Witnesses and other parties who attend tribunals normally have legal representation with them.

Although tribunals are quasi-judicial in manner, and tend to be chaired by sitting or retired judges, they do not pass judgments or hand out sentences. Instead, they make findings of fact and present interim and final reports to the Houses of the Oireachtas, which established them. These reports should contain recommendations on how to prevent the issue under investigation from being repeated, and may even lead to law reform. Importantly, statements made at a tribunal cannot be used in evidence against a person in criminal proceedings. They may however lead to further investigations by other means, which may result in criminal or civil proceedings.

Examples of tribunals of inquiry that have been established in recent years are given in Table 15.1 (many are also known by the name of their chairperson).

Other forms of investigation

Apart from tribunals of inquiry, other forms of investigation exist such as non-statutory inquiries (which cannot compel witnesses to attend) and commissions of investigation (which are chaired by barristers and can hear evidence in private). As noted in Chapter 6, Oireachtas committees can also engage in investigations within certain defined parameters.

The Prison Service

Prior to independence, Irish prisons were administered by the General Prisons Board, which had been founded in 1877. Post-1922, the newly established Department of Justice absorbed the functions of this board, and the management of prisons remained part of the remit of the department for the following decades. In 1985, the Report of the Committee of Inquiry into the Penal System (also known as the

Table 15.1. *Some tribunals of inquiry*

Name of tribunal	Year of establishment	Status
Tribunal of Inquiry into the Beef Processing Industry (Beef Tribunal)	1991	Final report presented in 1994
Tribunal of Inquiry into the Blood Transfusion Service Board (Finlay Tribunal)	1996	Final report presented in 1997
Tribunal of Inquiry (Dunnes Payments) (McCracken Tribunal)	1997	Final report presented in 1997
Tribunal of Inquiry into Certain Planning Matters and Payments (Mahon Tribunal)	1997	Inquiry ongoing as of May 2008
Tribunal of Inquiry into Payments to Politicians and Related Matters (Moriarty Tribunal)	1997	Inquiry ongoing as of May 2008
Tribunal of Inquiry into the Infection with HIV and Hepatitis C of Persons with Haemophilia and Related Matters (Lindsay Tribunal)	1999	Final report presented in 2002

Whitaker Report) supported the concept of a 'separate executive entity' to manage the state's prisons. However, it was another 10 years before the issue of a prisons agency was returned to.

In 1996 the government approved the establishment of an entity to run the prison service, and an expert group was appointed to review how this entity would operate in practice. This expert group recommended that the new body be called the Irish Prison Service and that it would relieve the Minister for Justice from the need to be involved in the daily running of prisons. An interim board for the agency was established in 1999 and today the Prison Service remains as an executive agency within the department. The Prison Service is responsible for managing 16 institutions, including those for juvenile offenders.

The work of the Prison Service is overseen by the Office of Inspector of Prisons. The inspector is charged with ensuring that the quality, standards and management of prisons are acceptable, and reports annually to the minister. The office-holder is independent of the Prison Service.

The Probation Service

Alongside the Prison Service, a Probation Service exists to facilitate court decisions to place offenders on probation supervision or community service rather than in prison, and to help offenders reintegrate into society and avoid reoffending. As part of the Department of Justice, Equality and Law Reform, the work of the service is achieved through a regional network of Probation Officers (as well as Community Service Supervisors) throughout the state. The Probation Service also supervises prisoners on temporary release and sex offenders over a period following their release from prison where a post-release supervision order is imposed.

16

An Garda Síochána

Having a police force to uphold law and order, prevent and limit crime, and provide security for citizens is a common desire of contemporary governments, democratic or otherwise. In fact, the concept of a police force is a relatively recent one when compared with other elements of the state apparatus, and emerged in tandem with the idea of nation-building and the need to maintain order. Today, how police forces perform their work has come to be one of the most important elements in gauging the state's relationship with its citizens. In Ireland, the relationship between the police service, the government and the people has been reformulated following recent legislation, in particular the Garda Síochána Act, 2005.

Upon the establishment of the Irish Free State, the (unarmed) Garda Síochána or 'Guardians of the Peace' came into existence, taking over the functions of the (armed) Royal Irish Constabulary and coexisting with the Dublin Metropolitan Police (DMP). The DMP amalgamated with An Garda Síochána in 1925. From then until the 1960s, the number of Gardaí and Garda stations in operation was relatively low, and it was not until the 1970s, with an increase in crime and the impact of the civil strife in Northern Ireland, that the numbers of full-time police officers passed 7,000. The numbers have continued to grow since then due to a variety of pressures (not least consistent political demands for more Gardaí 'on the beat'); the figure for 2007 stood at almost 14,000 sworn officers (including approximately 1,000 recruits) and over 2,000 civilians working within a network of approximately 700 Garda stations and with a fleet of over 2,200 vehicles. Since 1964, Garda training has taken place at the Garda Síochána College in Templemore, Co. Tipperary.

Structure of An Garda Síochána

The most senior position in the Gardaí is that of Garda Commissioner. Upon the establishment of the service, the Commissioner was responsible not to an independent police authority but directly to the Minister for Justice, who provided funding for the Gardaí. Since the Garda Síochána Act, 2005, the Commissioner is no longer appointed by the minister but by the government. Today, the Commissioner works closely with the Minister for Justice, Equality and Law Reform, who is responsible to the Oireachtas for the work of the force. The Garda Commissioner is assisted by two Deputy Commissioners – one concerned with operations and one with strategic and resource management – who in turn oversee the work of a number of Assistant Commissioners, to whom greater responsibilities have been devolved in recent years. There is also a Chief Administrative Officer who holds a rank equivalent to that of a Deputy Commissioner.

In order to organise the policing work of the Gardaí nationally, the county is divided into six regions, each of which is commanded by a Regional Assistant Commissioner. They are the:

• Dublin Metropolitan Region
• Southern Region
• Western Region
• Eastern Region
• Northern Region
• South Eastern Region.

Assistant Commissioners also exist for managing specialist areas such as traffic, and crime and security.

Each region is split into divisions, each managed by a Chief Superintendent who reports to his or her respective Assistant Commissioners. The divisions are broken into districts commanded by a Superintendent and a number of Inspectors, and the districts are divided into sub-districts, normally with a Sergeant assuming responsibility. The structure is given in Table 16.1. The service also employs a number of civilian staff who are recognised as civil servants of the government.

Functions of An Garda Síochána

Section 7(1) of the 2005 Garda Síochána Act states that the function of the service is to provide policing and security services for the state with the objective of:

Table 16.1. *Structure of An Garda Síochána*

Rank	Remit
Garda Commissioner	National
Deputy Garda Commissioner	
Regional Assistant Commissioners	Regional or specialist/ functional areas
Chief Superintendent	Division
Superintendent	District
Inspector	
Sergeant	Sub-district
Garda	
Garda Reserve	
Traince Garda	

- preserving peace and public order
- protecting life and property
- vindicating the human rights of each individual
- protecting the security of the state
- preventing crime
- bringing criminals to justice, including by detecting and investigating crime
- regulating and controlling road traffic and improving road safety.

Prior to the Garda Síochána Acts, 2005 to 2007, the Department of Justice had traditionally been very involved in the detailed day-to-day management of policing issues. For example, the Accounting Officer function for Garda expenditure was undertaken by the department. However, as the activities and demands on the force expanded in recent years, it was increasingly evident that the role of the department needed to become more strategic. These new Acts provided the basis for a new accountability relationship between An Garda Síochána, the minister and the department.

Under the Act (Section 26), the role of the Garda Commissoner is to:

- direct and control the Garda Síochána
- manage and control generally the administration and business of the service
- advise the minister on policing and security matters.

For example, the Garda Commissioner adopted more of the management functions such as the Chief Accounting Officer role, and responsibility for civilian employees has also been transferred from the department. Significantly, the Commissioner must 'account fully' for any aspect of his or her role to the Secretary General of the Department of Justice, Equality and Law Reform (Section 40).

Every three years, the Garda Commissioner presents a strategic policing plan to the minister for his or her agreement, who in turn places a copy of the plan before the Houses of the Oireachtas. The Commissioner must also prepare annual policing plans for the minister.

The department continues to play a key role in advising the minister on policing issues, in providing strategic direction to the Garda Síochána and in the development of secondary legislation governing recruitment, promotion, secondment, discipline and other issues within the Garda Síochána.

Within the Garda Síochána itself, the modernisation agenda has seen the creation of new posts such as Chief Administrative Officer, Director of Human Resources and Communications Director. Reflecting a greater 'civilianisation' of the force, some of these new posts have been filled by non-Gardaí.

Specialist support units

A number of specialist support units are involved in An Garda Síochána's investigation work, including the following.

Criminal Assets Bureau
The Criminal Assets Bureau was established as a statutory agency in 1996. It contains personnel not only from the Gardaí, but also from the Revenue Commissioners and the Department of Social, Community & Family Affairs. The role of the bureau is to identify assets derived from criminal activity, and to prevent criminals from accruing any benefit from those assets; it may repossess property if necessary. It has the power to apply a range of revenue, proceeds of crime and social welfare legislation in the course of its work, and to date has returned several million euro to the Exchequer.

Garda National Drugs Unit
The Garda National Drugs Unit was established in 1995 and is principally concerned with combating the trafficking of drugs. It is also

engaged in seizing drugs and in the prosecution of persons involved in their sale and distribution.

Garda Bureau of Fraud Investigation

The Garda Bureau of Fraud Investigation was also created in 1995. It provides a national focal point for intelligence and information on fraud. As well as dealing with money laundering, counterfeiting and computer-related fraud, the bureau is concerned with the more serious cases of commercial and financial fraud.

National Bureau of Criminal Investigation

The National Bureau of Criminal Investigation was established in 1997. Its main areas of concern are serious criminal matters, including organised crime, murder, sexual assaults, theft of such items as cars, art and antiques, and racketeering. In 2008 an Organised Crime Unit was established within its remit. The bureau works with local Gardaí, state agencies and international police organisations such as Europol (the European Law Enforcement Organisation) and Interpol (the International Criminal Police Organisation).

Special Detective Unit

Previously known as the Special Branch, the Garda Special Detective Unit is distinguished from the rest of An Garda Síochána by the fact that many of its members are armed. The unit is involved in a wide range of activities including surveillance of subversive and extremist groups, protection of high-profile state representatives and VIPs, and investigating certain criminal and terrorist activities.

The unit is also involved in providing security for witnesses in court cases as required, as well as for cash deliveries to banks and other institutions. It contains a smaller team known as the Emergency Response Unit, which was established in 1987 and may be called on to provide armed support assistance in serious criminal or terrorist situations involving firearms.

Garda National Immigration Bureau

The Garda National Immigration Bureau deals with immigration matters as they arise in the course of police work, and its personnel work in ports and airports. The bureau works closely with the Irish Naturalisation and Immigration Service, which is part of the Department of Justice, Equality and Law Reform. It has responsibility for border control, deportations and issues relating to trafficking and illegal immigration.

Other offices

Other offices within An Garda Síochána are concerned with providing logistical and administrative support. They include the Garda Technical Bureau, the Garda Research Unit, the Transport Section and the Command and Control Centre where all emergency calls are routed and dealt with.

Garda Reserve

As part of the Garda Síochána Act, 2005, a Garda Reserve was established and in 2006 an upper limit of 1,500 members was agreed by the Cabinet. Though not granted the full range of powers extended to Gardaí, members of the Garda Reserve work alongside and assist the Gardaí in the performance of such duties as foot patrol, monitoring CCTV, neighbourhood policing and some security duties. They also have some limited powers in relation to traffic, public order and crime, and can arrest persons in certain circumstances.

Joint Policing Committees

As noted in previous chapters, the concept of stakeholder participation has been extensively applied to public service reforms in Ireland. In the area of policing, Sections 35 and 36 of the 2005 Act provided for joint policing committees, which 'serve as a forum for consultations, discussions and recommendations on matters affecting the policing of the local authority's administrative area'.

While the committees do not discuss criminal cases or such matters, it is envisaged that they would provide for greater communication between Gardaí, local authorities and other stakeholders concerning levels and reasons for antisocial behaviour, disorder and crime, and how best to tackle them. The Joint Policing Committees submit a report annually to the local authority, Garda Commissioner and minister.

Garda Síochána Inspectorate

The 2005 Act provided for a three-member Garda Síochána Inspectorate. One of the members is known as the Chief Inspector. Section 117 describes the purpose of the inspectorate as being to:
    ensure that the resources available to the Garda Síochána are used so

as to achieve and maintain the highest levels of efficiency and effectiveness in its operation and administration, as measured by reference to the best standards of comparable police services.

In other words, the inspectorate seeks to promote best practice in all aspects of police work in Ireland. The inspectorate may be called on by the Minister for Justice, Equality and Law Reform to report on specific elements of police work in Ireland. The reports of such inquiries are made directly to the minister.

Garda Ombudsman Commission

One of the more innovative features of the 2005 Act was the establishment of the three-person Garda Ombudsman Commission. The role of this office is to provide an independent mechanism for investigating complaints made against Gardaí (although Gardaí may still be involved in the actual process, under the management of the commission). This function had previously been performed internally by the Garda Complaints Board.

The members of the commission are appointed by the President following their recommendation to both Houses of the Oireachtas by the government. The commission has extensive powers to investigate Garda activities and receive information.

17

The Defence Forces

As well as having a civilian policing apparatus, most states also retain a military service of some kind which can be called on to enforce government rule or to defend the state from attack. While Ireland is militarily neutral, the Defence Forces (Óglaigh na hÉireann) play an important national and international role. For many years the two key functions of the Defence Forces were to 'defend the national territory' and to 'aid the civil power'. More recently, the task of international peacekeeping has been added to these duties, and Irish soldiers have served under the United Nations flag in many trouble spots around the globe.

The President of Ireland is the supreme Commander of the Defence Forces. However, day-to-day responsibility for military command is exercised by the Minister of Defence on behalf of the government.

At the head of the Defence Forces is the Chief of Staff, who is responsible to the minister for all aspects of the Forces' work and functioning, as well as providing military advice to the government. The Chief of Staff is assisted by two Deputy Chiefs of Staff, one concerned with military operations and the other with support (logistics and finance).

The Chief of Staff and the two deputies, as well as the Secretary General for the Department of Defence and the Minister of State at the Department of Defence, form the Council of Defence. This body supports the Minister for Defence in his role as the authority responsible for the Irish military by virtue of the Defence Act, 1954.

In 2005 the first Ombudsman for the Defence Forces was appointed. The Ombudsman independently investigates complaints made by members and former members of the Defence Forces.

The Defence Forces comprise the Permanent Defence Forces (PDF – see Figure 17.1) and the Reserve Defence Forces (RDF). The PDF consists of three elements:

- the Army
- the Naval Service
- the Air Corps.

Figure 17.1. *Structure of the Permanent Defence Forces*

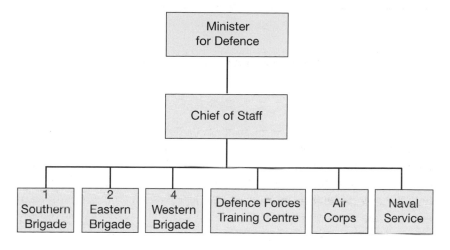

The Army

By international standards the Irish army is comparatively small; the regular force consists of a single division of approximately 8,500 personnel. There is also a reserve force that may be called upon to assist the army in the event of a military emergency. The division is subdivided into three brigades, each of which has a geographical basis and is commanded by a General Officer Commanding (Brigadier General) who has his or her authority delegated from the minister. The three brigades are:

- 1st Southern Brigade
- 2nd Eastern Brigade
- 4th Western Brigade.

Within the army are nine specialist sections or 'corps'. These include the Engineering Corps, Medical Corps, Artillery Corps, and the largest corps, Infantry.

Training in the Defence Forces is provided in the Curragh by the Defence Forces Training Centre, which is commanded by a General Officer Commanding. The Centre operates three separate colleges – Military College, Combat Support College and Combat Service Support College.

In terms of personnel, there are two 'streams' or rank structures for members of the Defence Forces – non-commissioned ranks and commissioned ranks. The former enter the Defence Forces as recruits or apprentices and once their training is completed, they remain as private soldiers. In ascending order, the principal non-commissioned ranks in the army are:

- Recruit or Apprentice
- Private
- Corporal
- Sergeant
- Company Quartermaster Sergeant
- Company Sergeant
- Battalion Quartermaster Sergeant
- Battalion Sergeant Major.

Officers in the commissioned ranks normally begin their career as a Cadet, and once basic training is completed they receive a commission from the President and graduate to the position of Second Lieutenant. The ranks thereafter are:

- Second Lieutenant
- Lieutenant
- Captain
- Commandant
- Lieutenant Colonel
- Colonel
- Brigadier General
- Major General
- Lieutenant General.

The army can be called on to support the police in a variety of duties. For example, enhanced levels of co-operation between the army and An Garda Síochána were exercised from the 1970s until the 1990s along the border with Northern Ireland in response to internal security threats. The army also supports the police in performing such duties as escorting cash transits or providing security for sensitive court cases. In 1975 an small elite and highly trained corps was established within the army known as the Army Ranger Wing, or 'Rangers'. It deals with such issues as hostage-taking or other military operations requiring particular specialist skills.

Several thousand Irish soldiers have served on United Nations peacekeeping and humanitarian relief operations missions since Ireland joined the UN in 1955. These have ranged from the Lebanon to the Congo, Cyprus to East Timor, and more recently have included Chad.

The Naval Service

The Naval Service is based in Haulbowline, Co. Cork and has a flotilla of eight ships. By far the greater part of Irish territory is actually submarine, and the Naval Service operates over a considerable geographical area. It performs such duties as patrolling Irish waters for illegal importation of drugs or other materials and policing fishing activities by trawlers. The service also runs the Naval Service College. Responsibility for the work of the Naval Service is delegated from the Minister of Defence to the Flag Officer Commanding. As with the army, a reserve force known as the Naval Service Reserve trains men and women to supplement and aid the Naval Service.

The Air Corps

The Air Corps has its headquarters in Casement Aerodrome in Baldonnel, Co. Dublin and operates 11 different types of aircraft. As with the army brigades, its work is overseen by a General Officer Commanding. As well as the Air Corps Training College, the Air Corps consists of two operational and two support wings, and a Communication and Information Services Squadron. The Air Corps supports the other elements of the Defence Forces as well as the civil powers, for example in search and rescue missions.

18

Northern Ireland

The history and development of government and public administration within Northern Ireland is complex and contested. In this chapter, the Assembly, local government, health, education, justice, policing and other elements of the administration for its population of 1.7 million are considered in their contemporary context. An important development in this respect was the initiation in 2002 by the Executive of the Northern Ireland Assembly of a 'Review of Public Administration', which examined the arrangements in place for the delivery of local government, health and education services. It concluded the main aspects of its work in 2005 and its final recommendations were published in 2005–6. Where appropriate, these recommendations are considered below.

A useful starting point for understanding governance structures in Northern Ireland is the Good Friday (or Belfast) Agreement, which was facilitated by the British and Irish governments, signed by the majority of political parties in Northern Ireland in 1998, and subsequently approved by popular majority in a referendum in both parts of the island. At its heart are three mutually dependent institutional arrangements or 'strands':

- a representative and popularly elected 108-member Assembly, which would also contain an executive exercising devolved powers
- a North/South Ministerial Council
- a British–Irish Council focusing on enhanced 'East–West' relationships.

The Assembly

Following the signing of the Good Friday Agreement in 1998, power was devolved from Westminster to a unicameral Assembly in Stormont, which contains an Executive of ministers overseeing 11 departments. The Assembly conducts its work in a cross-community manner. As with other representative assemblies, it has its own standing orders and all speeches are addressed to an impartial Speaker. It has legislative authority for policy in several areas including health, agriculture, education and the environment. Since its first sitting, the Assembly has been suspended on four occasions – once in 2000, twice in 2001 and again in October 2002 before being restored in May 2007 following new elections. During the suspensions, 'direct rule' ministers, deriving their authority from London, have instead exercised power.

One of the more unusual aspects of the Assembly's functional design is the requirement that each MLA (Member of the Legislative Assembly) designate himself or herself as 'nationalist', 'unionist' or 'other'. This self-ascription supports two key organisational tools for decisions requiring weighted cross-community agreement – 'parallel consent' and 'a weighted majority'. In the former case, for a motion to pass, it must receive the support of a majority of those voting, including a majority of those designated nationalist and unionist. The latter requires the support of 60% of those voting on the motion, and must include at least 40% from both the nationalist and unionist parliamentary groupings. Party representation in the Assembly is given in Table 18.1.

Table 18.1. *Party representation in the Assembly*

Party	1998 Election	2003 Election	2007 Election
Democratic Unionists	20	30	36
Sinn Féin	18	24	28
Ulster Unionists	28	27	18
Social Democratic and Labour Party	24	18	16
Alliance	6	6	7
Others	12	3	3

The Assembly also operates 10 committees, each with a Chair and Deputy Chair. The principal role of each committee is to oversee the work of the department to which it is aligned, as well as to engage in policy development and consultation. They also have particularly strong powers with respect to the legislative process. As part of the complex arrangements designed to maximise consensual decision-making, the chair and vice-chair of the statutory committees are drawn from the unionist and nationalist blocs respectively (or vice versa), and neither can be from the same party as the respective minister.

A separate committee known as the Committee for the Office of the First Minister and Deputy First Minister (prior to 2007 known as the Committee of the Centre) considers the work of that office, although it does not have full oversight capacity in respect of the office.

Apart from this committee, six standing committees have been established to engage in cross-departmental work. They are the Committees on Public Accounts, Audit, Business, Procedures, Standards and Privileges, and the Assembly and Executive Review Committee. To facilitate the work of the Assembly and its committees, there is an Assembly Commission which oversees all aspects of administration, services and staffing.

The Assembly elects an Executive from among its membership. At the apex of the Executive is the combined 'Office of the First Minister and Deputy First Minister'. In order to ensure representation of as many political voices as possible in the executive, ministers are nominated according to the d'Hondt electoral formula rather than being allocated to the party or parties that control a majority of seats, as occurs in other legislative arenas. Therefore since 2007 the four largest parties have held the ministerial portfolios in the following proportions:

- Democratic Unionist Party – 4
- Sinn Féin – 3
- Ulster Unionists – 2
- Social Democratic and Labour Party – 1

As of 2008, other than the Office of the First Minister and Deputy First Minister, the ten departments are:

- Department of Agriculture and Rural Development
- Department of Culture, Arts and Leisure
- Department of Education
- Department for Employment and Learning
- Department of Enterprise, Trade and Investment
- Department of the Environment
- Department of Finance and Personnel
- Department of Health, Social Services and Public Safety
- Department for Regional Development
- Department for Social Development.

These are staffed by the Northern Ireland Civil Service (NICS), an independent organisation established in 1921 and legally separate from the United Kingdom Home Civil Service. The Assembly also receives reports from the Northern Ireland Ombudsman, who is independent of both it and the Executive in terms of the investigation of complaints and allegations of maladministration.

North/South Ministerial Council

The second strand of the 1998 Agreement was a new North/South Ministerial Council. In plenary format, it comprises ministers from the Irish government and the Northern Ireland Executive, and its existence is tied to that of the Assembly, i.e. one cannot function without the other. The role of the council is to develop and take action of areas of mutual concern and cooperation on the island. It has a joint secretariat based in Armagh which comprises civil servants from both jurisdictions. As well as plenary meetings of ministers, the council can meet in sectoral format (to discuss institutional and cross-sectional issues).

In order to develop the work of the council, a number of Implementation Bodies have also been established whose role is to implement policies agreed by ministers in the council. There are currently six such bodies:

- Waterways Ireland
- North/South Language Body
- Food Safety Promotion Board
- Trade and Business Development Body
- Foyle, Carlingford and Irish Lights Commission
- Tourism Ireland Ltd.

The Implementation Bodies are staffed by civil servants from both jurisdictions, and the North/South Ministerial Council may establish new Implementation Bodies once agreement is forthcoming from both the Oireachtas and the Assembly. As well as the Implementation Bodies, there are six further non-statutory 'areas of co-operation' in which the council can develop cross-border or all-island work programmes. These are health, transport, tourism, agriculture, education and environment policy. Outside of the council, in areas such as energy and communications, there are also enhanced levels of co-operation between the two jurisdictions.

British–Irish Council[53]

The third and final strand in the institutional architecture created under the Good Friday Agreement is the British–Irish Council. This consists of representatives of the Irish and British governments, the Assemblies of Wales, Scotland and Northern Ireland, and the devolved institutions of the Isle of Man and the Channel Islands. The role of the British–Irish Council is to provide a forum for mutual co-operation and interaction on matters of concern including drugs, transport and the knowledge economy. It meets in summit format at least once a year and decisions are made by consensus among all bodies represented. The Secretariat for the Council is shared between the Office of the Deputy Prime Minister in Britain and the Irish Department of Foreign Affairs, but at the time of writing work is under way to provide a full-time secretariat.

The Secretary of State and the Northern Ireland Office

As noted above, the Assembly and Executive have jurisdiction over a wide range of issues. Responsibility for certain matters including taxation, security and justice, however, remains in the hands of the Secretary of State for Northern Ireland, a member of the British Cabinet. The position of Secretary of State has been in place since 1972, and he or she retains power over 'excepted and reserved matters', i.e. issues that have not been devolved to the Assembly. However, at the time of writing it is envisaged that further powers will be devolved to the Assembly. The Secretary of State is assisted by a minister of state (also a member of the British government), who is responsible for issues including criminal justice, security and policing, prisons and elections.

The Secretary of State and minister of state are supported by the Northern Ireland Office (NIO) and are responsible for the functioning of that office. The NIO is technically a department of the United Kingdom Civil Service rather than part of the Northern Ireland Civil

---

[53] The British-Irish Council should not be confused with the British–Irish Interparliamentary body established in 1990, which today consists of members of the Oireachtas and British Houses of Parliament, as well as representatives from the Scottish Parliament, National Assembly for Wales, Northern Ireland Assembly and elected assemblies of the Isle of Man, Guernsey and Jersey (www.biipb.org).

Service, and so its staff are seconded from the Department of Finance and Personnel. The NIO consists of five directorates and a range of associated bodies. The directorates are:

- Political
- Policing and Security
- Criminal Justice
- Information Service
- Central Services.

Executive agencies within the remit of the NIO include the Northern Ireland Prison Service, Compensation Agency, Forensic Science Agency and Youth Justice Agency.

Policing

Following the work and final report of the Independent Commission on Policing (the Patten Commission), which involved an extensive consultation process across Northern Ireland during 1998–9, the Police Service of Northern Ireland (PSNI) was created. The work of the PSNI is overseen by the Policing Board, and the Chief Constable is held to account by the board for the service's performance in relation to annual policing plans as well as a three-year strategy. The Policing Board, established in 2001, has 19 members of which nine are appointed by the Secretary of State and the remainder by the political parties. The Board also appoints independent members to the 26 District Policing Boards (see below).

The main policing work of the PSNI is based around eight District Command Units known as Districts A to H, with Belfast City comprising two such districts. These eight units are divided equally into two regions – urban and rural – with an Assistant Chief Constable taking responsibility for each region. At the local level, policing in each district is overseen by a Chief Superintendent, and the districts are subdivided into areas headed by an Area Commander Chief Inspector. There are 29 policing areas in all, and each has a District Policing Partnership with the exception of Belfast, which has one combining its four areas. As well as the rural and urban regions there are Assistant Chief Constables with responsibility for the other constituent departments of the PSNI, including crime operations, criminal justice, crime support and operational support. The Police Service also has finance, media and HR units.

The 26 District Policing Partnerships (DPPs) were established in 2003 following the recommendation of the Independent Commission on Policing and the subsequent Police (Northern Ireland) Act of 2000. Apart from local community representatives appointed to each DPP by the Policing Board, membership is made up of elected councillors nominated by their respective councils. DPPs vary in size but must consist of 15, 17 or 19 members in total. Their role includes representing community views on policing to the PSNI area commanders and making inputs to the local policing plans. The proposed reduction in the number of district council areas (see below) will require changes to the DPP structure.

The Police Ombudsman for Northern Ireland provides an independent complaints system for the public in relation to policing matters, and has extensive powers to initiate investigations as required.

Justice

The Northern Ireland Courts Service facilitates the conduct of the business of the courts system, which is similar to that of England and Wales. The most common courts are the Magistrates' Courts, which have jurisdiction over civil cases such as personal injury, discrimination and consumer dispute; and minor criminal matters. They are considered by a judge. Above the Magistrates' Courts are the County Courts, which have both civil and criminal jurisdictions. Appeals on civil issues coming before the Magistrates' Court can go for a full re-hearing in the County Court or, on occasion, to the Court of Appeal. Criminal cases appealed from the Magistrates' Courts can also be heard in the County Court, or in more serious cases in the Crown Court. The Crown Court normally has a jury, unless the offence is considered a 'scheduled offence' and the case is thus heard without one.

The next most senior court in Northern Ireland is the High Court, which hears appeals in relation to major civil cases, including divorce, adoption, (large) compensation claims, contested wills and bankruptcy. When the High Court hears criminal appeals it sits under the guise of the Crown Court. Appeals from the High Court or Crown Court go to the Court of Appeal. Further appeals from there are heard in the House of Lords. Recourse to the European Court of Justice is possible after this.

There are also a number of legal agencies that have counterparts in the Republic (see Chapter 15). The NIO funds the Crown Solicitors Office and the Public Prosecution Service. The Crown Solicitors Office represents the interests of the Crown in Northern Ireland, while the Public Prosecution Service, established in 2005, is responsible for prosecuting all criminal cases. There is also a Criminal Justice Inspectorate, which has a role in inspecting all offices and work systems involved in the criminal justice system, with the exception of the Courts. Its remit includes, for example, the Northern Ireland Prison Service, the Police Ombudsman and the Youth Justice Agency. The 11 government departments have their legal affairs managed by a branch of the civil service.

Local government

Local government structures in Northern Ireland and the Republic have common origins, and hence much of the language and institutions are recognisable either side of the border. For example, both Belfast and Cork acquired the position of Lord Mayor in 1900 and local authorities north and south are referred to as councils. However, while county boundaries continue to largely determine the jurisdiction of most local authorities in the Republic, a series of reforms during 1972–3 replaced Northern Ireland's 73 local authorities (including county councils and urban district councils) with 26 district councils. These reforms substantially stripped local government of its powers. A number of the councils – Belfast, Derry, Armagh, Lisburn and Newry – have either retained or recently been granted city status. Further consolidation is planned as the Review of Public Administration envisaged that the existing 26 councils would be replaced by a smaller number of 'super-councils', each with a greater range of devolved responsibilities. At the time of writing, a proposal for 11 local authorities has been put before the Assembly for approval.

Unlike the Republic of Ireland, homeowners in Northern Ireland pay 'rates' – this is effectively a local property tax. It is composed of a district rate, which is struck by district councils and funds local services, and a regional rate, which is set by the Assembly and funds other services including roads and hospitals provided by the departments. However, the vast bulk of public service funding comes in the form of an annual block grant from Westminster.

Health

There are also as in the Republic, general practitioners represent the smallest unit of the health care services, with over 350 practices employing one or more doctors. There are also 10 acute and six local hospitals serving a population of 1.7 million. In 2007, following the Review of Public Administration, 19 Health and Social Services Trusts were merged to create five new Health and Social Care Trusts and one Ambulance Trust. These trusts provide community care (including the hospitals) and related social services. Commissioning and overseeing health services, as well as providing information on services generally, are four Health and Social Services Boards. However, at the time of writing, these boards are scheduled to be replaced by a single Regional Health and Social Care Board. Apart from managing finances and performance issues, this new body will assume several functions of the Department of Health, Social Services and Public Safety, thus allowing the department to focus on strategic rather than operational issues.

There are also a number of health agencies in Northern Ireland, including the Blood Transfusion Service, the Social Care Council, the Regulation and Quality Improvement Authority and the Medical and Dental Training Agency. As part of the Review of Public Administration, it is proposed that a new Regional Public Health Agency be established to engage in health promotion and tackle health inequalities.

Education

Responsibility for setting education policy in Northern Ireland is divided between the Department of Education, which looks after pre-school, primary and second-level education, and the Department for Employment and Learning, which is concerned with third-level education and vocational training for those over compulsory school age (16). In addition, there are currently five Education and Library Boards (ELBs), which are responsible for the delivery of education, youth and library services within their particular geographical areas.

Primary and secondary education

There are a wide variety of primary and secondary schools in Northern Ireland. While a small number of privately funded schools exist, the vast majority are publicly funded with both capital and recurrent funding being provided by the Exchequer. In order to receive funding, schools are required to meet certain stipulations such as the adoption of a common curriculum, and to meet the educational standards set out by the Education and Training Inspectorate (ETI), which is responsible for overseeing the quality of education provided across all sectors. All schools are required to have an established Board of Governors with varying representation from the Department of Education and the ELBs, depending on which of the categories listed below applies.

In terms of ownership and governance, schools can be categorised into three groups, as follows.

Controlled

These schools are effectively owned and managed by the ELBs. Both teaching and non-teaching staff are directly employed by the ELBs. In general, these schools (both primary and secondary) were originally owned by the various Protestant denominations, and the churches are likely to have strong representation on their boards of governors. While there are a small number of controlled grammar schools, the vast majority are either primary or secondary schools.

Maintained

Like controlled schools, maintained schools are fully publicly funded. However, teaching staff are employed by the Catholic Council for Maintained Schools (CCMS), which is also responsible for bringing forward proposals on capital projects. Decisions on funding such projects remain with the Department of Education. Boards of governors will include representatives of the CCMS, the Catholic Church locally, the department and the ELBs. These are all either primary or secondary schools.

More recent additions to this category include the grant maintained integrated schools and the Gaelscoileanna or Irish-medium schools, which are overseen by Comhairle na Gaelscolaiochta.

Voluntary

While historically these schools would have had much more autonomy than either of the two categories above, successive education orders have sought to tie them more closely into the mainstream (controlled and maintained) schools by increasing the required representation for the department on their board of governors while simultaneously increasing the funding available for capital projects until almost all schools in this category are funded 100% for both capital and ongoing costs. Both teaching and non-teaching staff are employed by the schools and there is a more limited relationship with the ELBs, with all funding being provided directly by the department. In addition to receiving public funding, voluntary schools can raise 'voluntary contributions' from parents towards additional activities and facilities. Most if not all schools in this category are grammar schools, split broadly half and half between those that would be regarded as having a Catholic ethos and others.

Current policy developments
A number of major changes are taking place within education in Northern Ireland at present, including the proposed ending of academic selection, the establishment of a new overarching body, the Education and Skills Authority (to replace the five ELBs), and the introduction of major changes to the curriculum that would see schools co-operating to improve the choice of subjects available to students. In addition, a report in 2007 highlighted the need for major changes to the existing infrastructure to take account of both policy and demographic changes.

Children currently attend primary school up to the age of 11, when they can opt to submit themselves for a selection test, commonly known as the '11-Plus', which grades them in terms of academic ability. Schools will use this grade along with other criteria (such as proximity) to select its pupils for the following year. The issue of selection at 11 is very contentious in Northern Ireland, and a number of reviews have been carried out over the past 10 years as to whether the current arrangements should continue and, if not, what should replace them. At the time of writing proposals are in place for the ending of the 11-Plus and the introduction of a new system of self-selection at age 14.

Further/Third-level education
Two universities and a number of regional colleges offer further/third-level education in Northern Ireland. The universities are Queen's University Belfast and the University of Ulster. Queen's University was founded in 1845 and in 1999 incorporated two teacher-training colleges – St Mary's Unversity College (founded in 1900) and Stranmillis University College (founded in 1922). The University of Ulster was founded in 1984 following the merger of a number of existing third-level institutions, and today has campuses at Belfast, Coleraine, Jordanstown (Belfast) and Magee (Derry).

Prior to 2007, 16 autonomous further education colleges offered a wide range of higher and further education courses. These have since been merged into six regionally based colleges:

- Belfast Metropolitan College
- North West Regional College
- Northern Regional College
- Southern Regional College
- South West College
- South Eastern Regional College.

While the colleges can generate their own income by providing courses for adults and for private companies, most of their funding is provided by the Department for Employment and Learning, which sets the overall direction of the further education sector and monitors individual college performance against agreed targets. The introduction of minimum access entitlements for pupils at ages 14–16 and 17–18 is likely to increase the existing co-operation with schools.

19

The European Union

Ireland joined the European Economic Community (EEC) in 1973, after its accession had been ratified by the Irish people in a referendum held in 1972. Having begun as a community of six states, what is today referred to as the European Union (EU) has evolved into an organisation with 27 member states. It has a unique character, being neither a classic federal state like the United States nor an intergovernmental body like the United Nations, but instead a mixture of the two, with member states having agreed to delegate sovereignty over certain matters, but not others, to its autonomous institutions with their own binding law-making powers.

Those areas where the EU can legislate are identified in various Treaties that have provided critical points in the development of the Union. These include the 1957 Treaty of Rome, which founded the EEC, as well as the Single European Act, which entered into force in 1987, the Maastricht Treaty in 1993, the Treaty of Amsterdam of 1997, and the Nice Treaty in 2003.

These treaties provide the essence of a 'constitution' that must be considered alongside national constitutions (such as Bunreacht na hÉireann) when law is made in member states. In recent years, an attempt was made to consolidate the provisions of these Treaties into a single codified text referred to as an EU Constitution but, despite initial agreement by EU leaders in 2004, this was never ratified after negative referendums in two member states (France and the Netherlands). After a 'pause for reflection' much of the substance of this (but not the form or the name) was incorporated in the Lisbon or Reform Treaty, signed by European leaders in 2007, and awaiting final ratification at time of writing.

The EU has no jurisdiction in areas not identified in the treaties, such as taxation. In areas such as education and health, the EU's role is limited; in others, such as agriculture, social policy, transport and the environment, the EU has considerable influence. The Treaty of Lisbon seeks to clarify the extent of the EU's remit by identifying areas where the EU has *exclusive* competence, *shared* competence (with member states) and merely a *supporting* role.

Overall, the remit of the EU has expanded in recent decades and the body of EU law that has resulted is known as the *acquis communitaire* (or simply the *acquis*). Today there are few government departments, state agencies or local government bodies that are not affected by the work of the Union. In this chapter we consider the principal institutions at the heart of the EU and some of the ways in which EU affairs affect Irish government and public administration.

The principal European Union institutions

The 'institutional triangle' at the heart of EU law-making consists of three core institutions:

- the European Commission
- the Council of Ministers
- the European Parliament.

Rather than representing a separation of powers, the three core institutions represent different interests within the Union. As detailed below, the Commission represents general collective interests; the Council represents national governments; and the Parliament represents the citizens of the EU who elect it. Together, these institutions are involved in the initiation, negotiation and final adoption of EU legislation, and of the EU budget.

The work of these bodies is supported by the European Court of Justice, which plays a fundamental role, and the European Court of Auditors. Other EU institutions and bodies considered below include the:

- European Central Bank
- European Court of Auditors
- European Investment Bank
- European Economic and Social Committee
- Committee of the Regions
- European Ombudsman.

There are also 33 European agencies scattered throughout the Union that are concerned with specific issues. Examples include the:

- European Aviation Safety Agency
- European Food Safety Authority
- European Centre for Disease Prevention and Control
- Executive Agency for Competitiveness and Innovation
- European Railway Agency.

One of these agencies is situated in Ireland – the European Foundation for the Improvement of Living and Working Conditions (EUROFOUND). Also, a decentralised department of the European Commission – the European Food and Veterinary Office – is located in Ireland.

The European Commission
The European Commission has several major tasks assigned to it arising from the various EU Treaties:

- proposing new legislation to the Parliament and Council
- administering and implementing EU policies
- acting as the guardian of EU law within member states
- representing the EU in international agreements
- drafting an EU budget
- administering certain financial packages such as the European Development Fund and the European Social Fund.

The European Commission is headed by 27 political appointees known as Commissioners, including the President of the Commission. The President is appointed by a majority vote of the European Parliament following nomination by the European Council. The Commission as a whole is then subject to an overall vote of approval by the Parliament. While each member state appoints one Commissioner, they are meant to take decisions in the interests of the Union rather than their country of origin. Ireland's current Commissioner is Charlie McCreevy, who holds the Internal Market and Services portfolio. If the Lisbon Treaty is ratified, a system of equal 'rotation' between member states, big and small, will allow for a maximum of 18 commissioners from the 2014 Commission onwards.

Each Commissioner is given a portfolio but is expected to be aware of the principal issues affecting other portfolios at the weekly meetings of the Commission (known as the 'college') in Brussels. It is possible for the European Parliament to pass a motion of censure that would result in the resignation of the Commissioners, and the Commission President has the power to request the resignation of any of his or her Commissioners.

The Commission is staffed by over 23,000 personnel, a significant number of whom are involved in the translation of documents in the various working languages of the Union. The staff work in departments known as Directorates-General (DGs), each of which is headed by a Director-General. As each DG is the responsibility of a Commissioner, each Director-General must work closely with his or her Commissioner and their personal 'cabinet' of advisers. Given that there are more DGs than Commissioners, some Commissioners have responsibility for a number of DGs.

One of the most important roles of the Commission is in respect of its 'right of initiative' *vis-à-vis* EU legislation. This allows it to propose new laws to the Parliament and Council. This normally occurs after extensive consultation with the various governing authorities in member states (including national parliaments), interest groups and the general public. To aid it in its work, the Commission utilises a number of committees that are composed of civil servants and specialists in the subject area from the member states.

European legislation often provides for detailed implementing or adaptation measures to be adopted by the Commission to deal with technical issues related to EU law. In order to conduct this aspect of its work, the Commission uses another type of committee known as 'comitology' committees, which are composed of officials and/or experts from the member states. The Council, and now increasingly the European Parliament as well, is given a role in scrutinising these measures, or even asking that they be amended or replaced by other measures.

As the principal oversight body within the Union, the Commission is also charged with ensuring that member states adhere to the various rules established under EU Treaties. In this role, its principal source of information is complaints received from interest groups and individual citizens within the Union. The work of the various EU and national agencies as well as the media assists in this process. The ultimate sanction at the disposal of the Commission is to refer infringements of EU law by a member state to the European Court of Justice, which has the power to impose fines in the event of a persisting infringement. However, before this will happen the member state will be given ample opportunity to attempt to rectify the situation.

The Commission also allocates large sums of money to member

states, such as through the EU Structural Funds programme. It must ensure that such funds are not wasted, and works closely with the European Court of Auditors in ensuring financial accountability. In order to receive Structural Funds, a member state must develop a National Strategic Reference Framework which demonstrates how it will spend them. Only when the framework has been agreed can the Commission proceed to provide funds.

Among its many other roles, the Commission represents the EU in some international matters, and particularly trade issues. It also has a role in respect of the distribution of the EU's development and humanitarian aid budget.

The Council of Ministers

Officially known since the Maastricht Treaty as the Council of the European Union, the Council of Ministers consists of the representatives (ministers) of governments from each member state, who are accountable to their respective parliaments and hence to citizens. Until recently, one of the principal roles of the Council of Ministers was to decide on the adoption or not of legislation proposed by the Commission. However, this power is increasingly shared with the European Parliament through the so-called co-decision procedure, which will become the ordinary legislative procedure if the Lisbon Treaty is ratified. Other powers of the Council include approving the EU budget (with the European Parliament) and concluding international agreements on behalf of the EU. It also has a role in relation to two issues of great importance to national governments – justice and home affairs, and common foreign and security policy.

While the Council takes its decisions as a single body, which ministers attend depends on the issue to be discussed. Since 2002, there have been nine 'configurations' of the Council, including:

- Agriculture and Fisheries
- Environment
- Employment, Social Policy, Health and Consumer Affairs
- Economic and Financial Affairs
- General Affairs and External Relations Council.

The Council meets in Brussels and sometimes Luxembourg, and European Commissioners with responsibility for the area under discussion also attend Council meetings. An important development in recent years has been that a number of Council meetings, which were previously held behind closed doors, have been held in public or online.

The Council of Ministers should not be confused with the European Council, which is a meeting (or 'summit') of the heads of government (or state) of each member state and the President of the Commission. Though not an institution of the Union in itself (although this would change with the Lisbon Treaty), the European Council is the most important gathering within the EU as its sets the future policy framework and direction of the Union. New Treaties such the Lisbon Treaty of 2007 are signed by the members of the European Council.

Just as civil servants help prepare material for their minister's Cabinet meetings in national settings, a vast amount of administrative work goes into the preparations for Council meetings. This is organised through committees or 'working groups' composed of civil servants from each member state, as well as an intermediate body known as COREPER – the committee (or collection) of permanent representatives from each member state.

All member states have their own permanent representation in Brussels. These 'perm reps' are a combination of civil servants from different departments and diplomats, and are headed by an official known as the Permanent Representative (a position equivalent to the rank of ambassador). The role of the Irish permanent representation is varied. First and foremost, it is expected to keep the government aware of developments in the EU that may affect Irish interests, domestic or otherwise. The permanent representation may also represent Ireland and its interests at a number of EU committees and working groups, or act as an intermediary between an EU institution and the Irish government. Members of the representation accompany ministers or Irish officials to Council or other meetings. The permanent representations from all member states communicate regularly with each other to determine the positions of various governments on different issues.

In order to pursue its work, the Council of Ministers depends on the work of COREPER,[54] which is facilitated by a large number of working groups that examine legislation emerging from the Commission. Member states are represented by civil servants at these meetings, or else by non-civil servants who have a particular relevant expertise. If a

---

[54] For agricultural issues, a separate body known as the Special Committee on Agriculture exists.

member state has a difficulty with a part of a proposal, it is noted as a 'reservation' to be addressed at a higher level. The flow of work is therefore as shown in Figure 19.1.

Figure 19.1. *Flow of work*

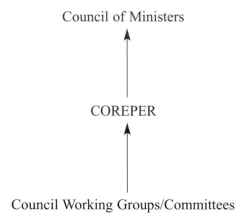

Council of Ministers

COREPER

Council Working Groups/Committees

Only contentious or unresolved issues reach the Council level – most issues are agreed either in the working groups or at COREPER level. Governments therefore place a lot of trust in their permanent representation, who must ensure that national positions are not unduly compromised in the development of EU legislation.

A small number of Council decisions can be taken by simple majority (i.e. at least 14 out of 27 votes). These are normally uncontentious areas. The vast majority of Council decisions are taken either by unanimity (any single member-state can veto a proposal) or by qualified voting majority (QMV). Considerable efforts are made to make decisions by consensus and to avoid cleavages between member states.

Currently, under QMV, each member state is assigned a number of votes; the total is 345. The distribution of votes is given in Table 19.1.

For a proposal to be successful under QMV, it requires the approval of a majority of member states and a minimum of 255 votes (over 70% of the total). Also, a member of the Council can request verification as to whether the combination of member states that led to the 255 votes constitutes at least 62% of the population of the EU. If not, the proposal cannot be adopted.

The Treaty of Lisbon proposes to change the definition of QMV

Table 19.1. *Shares of votes under QMV (a total of 232 votes is required for a proposal to pass)*

Country	Votes
Germany, UK, France, Italy	29
Spain, Poland	27
Romania	14
The Netherlands	13
Greece, Czech Republic, Belgium, Hungary, Portugal	12
Sweden, Austria, Bulgaria	10
Ireland, Denmark, Finland, Lithuania, Slovakia	7
Luxembourg, Latvia, Slovenia, Estonia, Cyprus	4
Malta	3
Total	*345*

from November 2014 onwards. Under the revised system, a qualified majority (or 'double majority') would be defined as 55% of the members, comprising at least 15 member states representing 65% of the EU's population. Also, a proposal can only be blocked if it is opposed by at least four member states. In almost 60 areas, the need for a unanimous vote will remain.

The Council currently has a *rotating Presidency*. This means that every six months the Presidency rotates between member states. The Presidency is a key organisational mechanism for the work of the Council, as the member state holding it is expected to facilitate and mediate discussions, as well as take up duties in respect of EU foreign policy. The work of the Presidency is assisted by the Council's permanent secretariat, which provides interpretative services and legal advice among other duties. The Council also has its own secretariat, which assists the Presidency in arranging meetings, writes up the minutes of meetings, provides interpretation and has a legal service to advise participants in meetings on legal questions.

The Lisbon Treaty, signed in 2007, proposes that a new position of President of the Council be created, the holder of which would be chosen by members of the European Council for a two-and-a-half-year term, renewable once. The rotating Presidency would, however, continue (in only slightly modified form) for many policy areas, with the exception of the Council of Foreign Ministers, which would be presided over by the High Representative for Foreign and Security Policy. This High Representative would be appointed by the Council (with the agreement of the President of the Commission) and would provide a voice for the EU in international affairs, dealing with issues such as development aid and trade. He or she would also chair a 'Foreign Affairs Council', whose functions are currently part of the General Affairs and External Relations Council (see above).

The European Parliament

The third key institution in the EU is the European Parliament. While for many years it was regarded as weaker in power and influence than the Commission and the Council, in recent times the Parliament has grown in authority. The Treaty of Lisbon envisages that it will gain further competences. It now has extensive legislative and budgetary powers, helps to elect the Commission, can say 'yes' or 'no' to enlargement and certain international agreements, and has a number of additional powers.

A European Assembly consisting of members of national legislatures who would be nominated to the European arena was provided for under the original agreements forming the European Economic Community. Direct elections to what became the European Parliament occurred for first time in 1979, and are held every five years – the next such elections will be in June 2009. There are currently 785 Members of the European Parliament (MEPs), elected within the 27 member states. The distribution of seats by country roughly corresponds to population sizes, and Ireland currently has 13 MEPs. The Treaty of Lisbon proposes to reduce the number of MEPs to 750 (plus a non-voting President), which means that Ireland's representation will be reduced to 12 MEPs.

Once elected, MEPs organise themselves within the parliament not according to nationality but in political groupings, just as occurs in national legislatures. While much of the work of the European Parliament is performed in committees, being a member of a transnational party is important as the distribution of committee memberships and of key jobs within the parliament is decided by the political groups. These party groupings (which must have more than 20 members to be recognised) and the memberships elected in 2004 are given in Table 19.2.

For a variety of reasons, the meetings and administration of the European Parliament are divided between Strasbourg, Brussels and Luxembourg. MEPs spend most of their time in the committees to which they are assigned. There are 20 standing committees in the European Parliament, including the:

Table 19.2. *Party groupings in the European Parliament*

Name	Number of MEPs (as of January 2008)	Number of Irish MEPs
European People's Party – European Democrats (EPP-ED)	288	5
Party of European Socialists (PES)	215	1
Alliance of Liberals and Democrats for Europe (ALDE)	101	1
Greens and European Free Alliance (G-EFA)	42	
European United Left – Nordic Green Left (GUE-NGL)	41	1
Union for Europe of Nations (UEN)	44	4
Independence and Democracy (IND/DEM)	24	1
Unattached (NI)	30	
Total	785	13

- Committee on Environment, Public Health and Food Safety
- Committee on Regional Development
- Committee on Foreign Affairs
- Committee on Employment and Social Affairs
- Committee on Culture and Education
- Committee on Industry, Research and Energy.

Legislation and other proposals forwarded to the parliament are directed to the relevant committee (or committees) for examination. The committee then appoints a *rapporteur* to write up the committee's views on the proposal, which is debated and if necessary redrafted by the committee before being sent to the full plenary session of the parliament. At this stage the parliament can accept, reject or amend the legislative text and/or resolution. Alternatively, it can refer it back to the committee for further examination. Temporary committees or sub-committees can also be established, and the Parliament has a number of delegations to which are assigned specific duties, including relations with other countries and international organisations.

The main work of the European Parliament can be categorised as oversight, legislative or budgetary. In relation to oversight, as noted above the Parliament retains the right to remove the college of Commissioners. The Parliament is also required to approve the Commissioners nominated by the President of the Commission, and appoints the European Ombudsman. MEPs can submit questions to the Council and Commission, and Commissioners and their officials will appear before the Parliament and its committees on a regular basis. It is not unusual for the Parliament to establish temporary committees of inquiry to investigate specific matters of concern. The Petitions Committee plays an increasingly visible role in looking at citizens' complaints from all over the EU.

The area where the Parliament has had its role significantly increased in recent years is that of legislation. While the Council traditionally held the power to approve or reject a range of Commission proposals, the Parliament has gained the power of 'co-decision' across a wide range of areas and can now amend or even veto most legislation it is not satisfied with. Co-decision means that the approval of both the Parliament and the Council is required for a Commission proposal to succeed. This involves bargaining between the two institutions (as well as with the Commission), and therefore gives the Parliament a greater influence in EU legislation. Co-decision occurs in relation to such matters as social exclusion, free movement and the environment. A few areas remain where the Parliament has a weaker legislative role, and is only consulted, but the Treaty of Lisbon would further reduce these.

Finally, in relation to budgets, the Parliament has a say over all aspects of the EU annual budget, and although its current powers can vary, its influence on the multi-annual budgetary perspectives is growing. In particular, the Parliament can influence the allocation of Structural Funds (for economic and social development, of which Ireland received over €900 million for the period 2007–13), funds for research and development and a host of other areas. It is also possible for the Parliament to reject the whole budget, and this has occurred in the past.

It should be noted that the European Parliament organises meetings between its committees and the counterpart committees of member states' national legislatures. In fact, the number of such meetings has more than quadrupled in the past 10 years.

European Union legislation

The discussion above of the three key EU institutions has noted their respective roles in relation to legislation. While the Parliament has only the status of a consultee on certain policy issues, in most cases it has the power of co-decision on Commission proposals along with the

Figure 19.2. *The co-decision process*

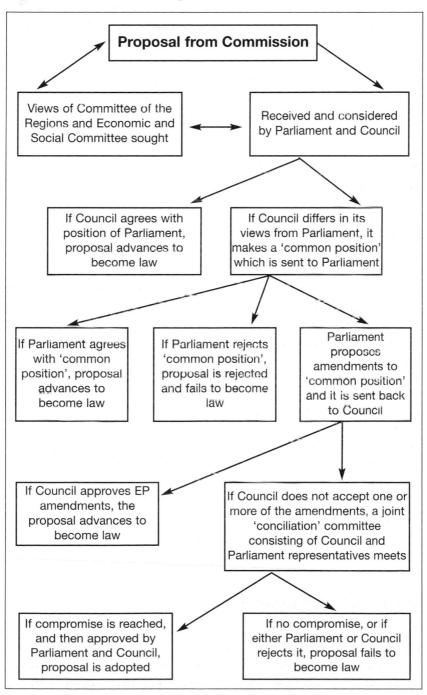

Council. An illustration of this process of co-decision is set out in Figure 19.2.

For member states and their legislatures, membership of the Union presents particular challenges to their remit as EU law is 'supreme' to domestic law, i.e. no national laws can be in conflict with EU law. There are in fact several different types of legislation within the Union – *regulations*, *directives* and *decisions*. While these three are legally binding measures, there are also non-legally-binding measures known as *recommendations* and *opinions*. In most cases, EU legislation must be *transposed* by member states, i.e. their national legislatures must pass legislation to make the provisions of the EU legislation applicable in their domestic setting.

Regulations are automatic EU law. They are directly applicable and binding on all member states on a specified date without the need for transposing legislation.

Directives are more common than regulations and allow member states greater flexibility. Rather than specifying in detail what a member state must do, directives set a goal to be achieved and require member states to transpose this goal into their national law. How the goal is achieved is therefore up to the member state, but often a deadline will be set in the legislation by which time the member state must have completed the transposition or face a fine. In Ireland, the European Communities Act, 2007 allows ministers to use existing Acts of the Oireachtas to create statutory instruments to implement EU law, once the Act in question relates to the same policy area.

While regulations and directives are applicable to all within the Union, decisions are directed at individual member states, organisations or even individuals. They are legally binding and, like directives, are flexible with regard to implementation.

Turning to the non-legally binding measures: recommendations express a detailed EU preference on an issue. An opinion is similar in that it represents an expression of commitment by the EU but does not have direct effect.

Alternatives to formal legislation are sometimes sought, such as voluntary agreements or a process known as the open method of co-ordination. This encourages peer-review between member states to identify best practice and non-legislative ways of achieving EU objectives.

Another recent trend has been towards the development of much more systematic impact assessment to accompany the presentation of new legislative proposals. Such impact assessment is meant to look at economic, social, environmental and other impacts, and to become an integral part of the EU legislative process. As noted in Chapter 8, regulatory impact analysis (RIA) has also been adopted in Ireland for the purpose of assessing the impacts of domestic regulations.

Managing and co-ordinating EU issues

Membership of the EU introduces considerable burdens on the governing institutions of member states, and each has devised methods of managing EU business. Irish representatives in the EU – whether within the permanent representation or elected MEPs – play an important role in supporting Irish interests and providing 'early warning' on forthcoming legislation. Similarly, knowledge and understanding of EU affairs is increasingly important for civil servants in the development of their career, and most can expect to spend time in Brussels or elsewhere representing their department at some stage.

At a political level, the role of the Oireachtas in scrutinising EU business has been augmented in recent years as a result of the European Union (Scrutiny) Act, 2002. Among its provisions, the Act requires ministers to brief the Joint Oireachtas Committee on European Affairs and other Oireachtas committees on the agenda of Council meetings that they are going to attend. Ministers are also expected to take cognisance of recommendations made by the Oireachtas and its committees in the course of their deliberations with counterparts from other EU member states. The Joint Oireachtas Committee on European Affairs has provisions allowing for MEPs from both the Republic and Northern Ireland to attend and take part in proceedings.

The Act also established a Sub-Committee on European Scrutiny that acted as a filter for the large volume of EU documents, which could if necessary be forwarded to the relevant sectoral committee depending on their importance and relevance. This has recently been turned into a full Joint Committee on EU Scrutiny. The committee's work has been aided by improvements in sending EU documents such as proposed legislation to national parliaments for consideration and comment at an earlier stage. The Lisbon Treaty proposes to enhance this process by giving national parliaments more background information, more time to feed in their views, and a new mechanism for objecting to proposals on the grounds of 'subsidiarity', i.e. that the proposal is an inappropriate one for action at EU level.

Departments are also expected to provide the relevant committees with briefings on proposed EU legislation in order to assist its deliberations. The EU Division within the Department of Foreign Affairs plays an important linkage role in all of this work. Also, within the Cabinet, there is a Sub-Committee on European Affairs chaired by the Taoiseach, and including the Ministers for Foreign Affairs, Finance and ministers from other portfolios as necessary. Also, there is currently a minister of state at the Department of the Taoiseach and the Department of Foreign Affairs with responsibility for European Affairs. The office-holder has a co-ordinating role and chairs the Interdepartmental Coordinating Committee on European Union Affairs.

Other EU institutions

European Court of Justice

The European Court of Justice (ECJ) is the judicial institution of the European Union. It is composed of the Court of Justice, the Court of First Instance and the Civil Service Tribunal. The Court of First Instance was established in 1989 to assist the ECJ in its workload by providing rulings on certain cases, and the Civil Service Tribunal was established in 2004 to rule on disputes involving the EU civil service. The ECJ sits in Luxembourg and is composed of 27 judges (one judge nominated by each member state), as well as eight advocates general who assist them in forming decisions. The judges are appointed for six years and elect a President from among their membership for a period of three years.

The ECJ serves to uphold EU Treaties, interpret EU law and ensure that EU law is implemented equally by member states. Cases are distributed between the judges, with one judge and advocate general assigned to each case. Over the years it has established important legal precedents such as the principle of supremacy, which determines that where provisions of EU law conflict with national law, EU law prevails. It hears cases during the full year. There are different categories of proceedings within the court's jurisdiction – preliminary rulings, proceedings relating to failure to fulfil obligations, proceedings for annulment and proceedings for failure to act. The ECJ also hears appeals on decisions made in the Court of First Instance. If ratified, the Treaty of Lisbon will provide the court with increased powers to impose fines on member states for breaches of EU law. Also, as the Lisbon Treaty proposes to give the European Charter of

Fundamental Rights legal status by recognising the rights, freedoms and principles set out in the charter, it will increase the jurisdiction of the court.

- *Preliminary rulings* – These proceedings occur when a member state's courts request clarification from the ECJ concerning interpretation of EU law in order to ensure that its national law is consistent with it. The decision of the ECJ is binding on all member states.
- *Proceedings relating to failure to fulfil an obligation* – These proceedings are normally brought by the Commission but may be brought by a member state. They occur in relation to the failure of a member state to fulfil an obligation under EU law. The ECJ may fix a fine on the member state for failing to address the issue subsequently.
- *Proceedings for annulment* – These actions occur when a community institution or member state (or sometimes an individual) seeks the annulment or cancellation of an EU law on the basis that it conflicts with the EU Treaties.
- *Proceedings for failure to act* – These proceedings occur when an EU institution fails to take action having been called upon to do so.

European Court of Auditors

The role of the European Court of Auditors (ECA) is to audit the accounts of the EU's institutions. It sits in Luxembourg, and each member state nominates an auditor to the court. Auditors hold their position for six years, and a President is elected from among them on a three-year basis. Most of the Court of Auditors' work concerns the budget of the Commission, and member states play an important role in managing the funding provided to them through the Commission (such as Structural Funds). The independence of the Court of Auditors is central to the successful performance of their work. Any irregularities it uncovers are forwarded to the European Anti-Fraud Office.

European Central Bank

The European Central Bank (ECB) was established in 1998 following years of negotiations that culminated in the adoption of the euro currency by a majority of member states. The ECB has a governing council that consists of the six members of the executive board as well as the governors of the national central banks from the fifteen euro-area countries. It normally meets twice a month. The ECB and the national central banks of the participating member states constitute the Eurosystem, which seeks to maintain price stability and to design and define monetary policy for the participating members. Monetary policy includes decisions relating to key interest rates (such as lending and deposit rates), the conduct of foreign exchange operations, management of the supply of reserves in the Eurosystem and the creation of guidelines for implementing these decisions. The Treaty of Lisbon proposes to formalise the position of the ECB by making it an institution of the EU.

European Investment Bank

The European Investment Bank (EIB) was established in 1958 to help finance initiatives consistent with the objectives of the then Treaty of Rome. Today it seeks to enhance economic and social integration within the EU through its borrowing and lending activities. The shareholders of the EIB are the 27 member states of the EU, and a minister from each state (usually the Finance Minister) is appointed to the Bank's board of governors. There is also a 28-member board of directors, with a director nominated by each member state along with a nominee of the Commission. The EIB manages the European Investment Fund, of which it is the majority shareholder alongside the European Commission. The fund is principally used for encouraging small and medium enterprises, though it is also the source of long-term loans for large capital projects. Internationally, the EIB is responsible for meeting the EU's obligations on development aid and cooperation. It is non-profit-making and is not funded by the EU; it raises the money to finance its activities on the international financial market.

European Economic and Social Committee

The European Economic and Social Committee (EESC) is a forum for EU civil society that meets in full plenary session about ten times per year. It has 344 members (nine of whom are from Ireland), who are nominated by member-state governments for a four-year term. Members represent 'employers', 'employees' or 'various interests' (including farming interests, NGOs and small and medium-sized enterprises). It provides opinions on many issues (such as environmental or social policy) to the EU institutions, in a consultative capacity, and the committee must be consulted by those institutions on certain matters specified under the EU treaties. The EESC can also offer 'exploratory opinions' to the Commission, which may lead to new legislative proposals by that body.

The work of the EESC is channelled through six sections:

- Agriculture, Rural Development and the Environment
- Economic and Monetary Union and Economic and Social Cohesion
- Employment, Social Affairs and Citizenship
- External Relations
- The Single Market, Production and Consumption
- Transport, Energy, Infrastructure and the Information Society.

Every two years a bureau of 37 members is elected by the committee to coordinate its work.

Committee of the Regions

In many EU countries, regional authorities hold considerable power, and prior to the establishment of the Committee of the Regions in 1994 had long sought a means for their views to be represented in the EU legislative process other than through national governments in the Council. The committee was a creation of the Maastricht Treaty and its structures resemble the EESC in many ways. There are also 344 members (mainly but not exclusively politicians, including nine from Ireland), who represent the local and/or regional levels of government in their country. They are appointed for a four-year term and, like the European Parliament, there are a number of political party groupings within the committee.

The main work of the committee is conducted through six commissions (including for example a Commission on Economic and Social Policy and a Commission for Sustainable Development). The committee elects a bureau of 60 members every two years to implement an agreed political programme. It is also an advisory body to the European institutions on a wide range of legislative issues; however, its views on EU legislation have no binding force. As with the EESC, there are certain specified areas in which the views of the committee must be sought. One of its main roles is to ensure that the principle of subsidiarity is adhered to, i.e. that decisions are taken at a level that is as close to citizens of the EU as possible.

European Ombudsman

The post of European Ombudsman was also provided for in the Maastricht Treaty, and was established in 1995. The office-holder is appointed by the European Parliament for a period of five years and is located in Strasbourg. The role of the Ombudsman is to act as an intermediary between EU citizens and the EU authorities (excluding the Court of Justice). The Ombudsman can also initiate an investigation independently and makes recommendations on eliminating malpractice in administration where it exists. The Ombudsman cannot act on his or her findings but instead reports to the parliament, which then makes a decision concerning actions.

20

Membership of international organisations

The Constitution states that 'Ireland affirms its devotion to the ideal of peace and friendly co-operation amongst nations founded on international justice and morality' (Art. 29.1). Apart from membership of the European Union and the British–Irish Council, therefore, Ireland has also successfully sought membership of a number of international organisations. The number of such organisations has grown in recent years. The more significant bodies to which Ireland has varying commitments are detailed below.

United Nations

The United Nations (UN) was formed in the aftermath of the Second World War in 1945 and Ireland joined in 1955. The UN is governed by a charter, which broadly describes the goals of the organisation as achieving international peace and security, developing relations and co-operation between nations, and promoting freedom and human rights. The General Assembly of the UN consists of representatives of 192 nations. The Security Council is one of the UN's most important institutions, consisting of five permanent members – the United States, United Kingdom, Russian Federation, China and France – and 10 non-permanent members. Ireland was a non-permanent member in 1962, 1981–2 and most recently in 2001–2. Other institutions of the UN include the Economic and Social Council and the International Court of Justice. The latter is situated in The Hague and settles legal disputes between states as well as providing legal advice to the UN.

Ireland is also a party to a number of agencies and organisations under the remit of the UN, such as the Food and Agriculture Organisation, the International Telecommunication Union, the International Labour Organisation and the United Nations Educational, Scientific and Cultural Organisation (UNESCO).

World Trade Organisation

The World Trade Organisation (WTO) was founded in 1995 in Geneva, and emerged from the General Agreement on Tariffs and Trade, which has been created in 1948. Ireland was a founder member of the WTO. At the apex of the organisation is the Ministerial Conference, where ministers from the 151 member states meet; this occurs at least once every two years. Between these meetings, the organisation's work is handled by a General Council, a Dispute Settlement Body and a Trade Review Body. As the structures suggest, the WTO provides a forum for trade negotiations and resolving trade disputes between nations, for monitoring the trade policies of national governments and other issues including intellectual property and transparency in government procurement. The work of the WTO is framed by agreements signed by a majority of its members. The current such agreements include a revised General Agreement on Tariffs and Trade and a General Agreement on Tariffs and Services.

World Health Organisation

The World Health Organisation (WHO) is also based in Geneva; since its establishment in 1948 its membership has grown to 193 states. It seeks to improve public health internationally and to provide for more collaboration on health matters between nations. The World Health Assembly, which meets annually, is the supreme decision-making body for the WHO and elects the Director-General. One of the WHO's best-known publications is the annual *World Health Report*, which provides detailed statistics and measures on health-related issues for each member state.

World Bank

The World Bank was formed in 1944 and was centrally involved in post-Second World War redevelopment through the International Bank for Reconstruction and Development (IBRD), which Ireland joined in 1957. Today, it consists of the IBRD and the International Development Association (IDA), and has a mandate involving tackling world poverty through the provison of loans, credit and grants to developing countries. It also produces the annual *World Development Report*. Other organisations within the World Bank group of which Ireland has membership include the International Centre for Settlement of Investment Disputes, the International Finance Corporation and the Multilateral Investment Guarantee Agency.

Council of Europe

Not to be confused with the European Council (see Chapter 19), the Council of Europe is a separate organisation based in Strasbourg, consisting of 47 European countries, including non-EU states in the Balkans and Eastern Europe as well as Russia. Founded in 1949, it has a separate membership and remit to the European Union. Its main aims are to advance the goals of the European Convention on Human Rights and to promote democracy and the rule of law. It also provides a forum for co-operation on issues of concern to member states. The decision-making body of the Council is the Committee of Ministers, which consists of the Foreign Ministers of the respective member states (or their deputies). There is also a parliamentary assembly of 636 members nominated from member states' parliaments, and a bicameral Congress of Local and Regional Authorities.

European Court of Human Rights

The European Court of Human Rights (ECHR), which is located in Strasbourg, is an institution of the Council of Europe. The task of the ECHR is to hear cases taken on the basis of the European Convention on Human Rights, which a large number of countries (both EU and non-EU) have signed.

European Bank for Reconstruction and Development

This bank was created in 1991 in order to help redevelop the former Communist states in Central and Eastern Europe, but has since expanded its work. Ownership of the bank is shared by 61 states, including Ireland, as well as the European Investment Bank (see Chapter 19) and the European Union. All are both members and shareholders. The bank borrows funds in the international markets and then invests in and offers loans to private businesses (and also some public enterprises) in the countries where it operates.

European Patent Organisation

The European Patent Organisation was founded in 1977 and Ireland joined in 1992. It consists of two bodies – the European Patent Office, which has a legal personality and to which Ireland is a contracting state, and the Administrative Council, to which Ireland appoints a representative. The Patent Office provides a focal point for inventors and companies that wish to patent products and services in the countries which are members. A European Patent Convention was signed in 2007 to help structure this work.

Further reading

General

For contrasting Irish government and public administration today with that of the 1960 and 1970s, the several editions of Jim O'Donnell's *How Ireland is Governed* (Dublin: Institute of Public Administration) are instructive. Basil Chubb's *Sourcebook of Irish Government* (2nd ed.; Dublin: Institute of Public Administration, 1983) provides an essential history of key documents in the development of the administration, while his *Government and Politics of Ireland* (2nd ed.; London: Longman, 1982) remains groundbreaking in its approach to politics, policy and policy-makers. Though increasingly outdated, a number of other works focusing solely or partially on Irish public administration include:

Barrington, T. J. (1980) *The Irish Administrative System.* Dublin: Institute of Public Administration.

Dooney, S. and O'Toole, J. (1998) *Irish Government Today* (2nd ed.). Dublin: Gill & Macmillan.

Hussey, G. (1995) *Ireland Today: Anatomy of a Changing State* (2nd ed.). Dublin: Penguin.

Due to a dearth of academic or analytical research on the broad chapter themes herein, several of the chapters in this volume relied on practitioners and official sources for information and data. For the remaining chapters the following texts were used and are recommended for more detailed research:

Bunreacht na hÉireann/The Constitution of Ireland

Constitution Review Group (1996) *Report of the Constitution Group.* Dublin: Stationery Office.

Farrell, B. (ed.) (1988) *De Valera's Constitution and Ours.* Dublin: Gill & Macmillan.

Keogh, D. and McCarthy, A. (2007) *The Making of the Irish Constitution, 1937.* Cork: Mercier Press.

Ryan, F. W. (2002) *Constitutional Law.* Dublin: Round Hall Sweet & Maxwell.

Dáil Éireann

Gallagher, M. (2005) 'Parliament' in J. Coakley and M. Gallagher, *Politics in the Republic of Ireland* (4th ed.). Oxford: Routledge/PSAI, pp. 211–242.

MacCarthaigh, M. (2005) *Accountability in Irish Parliamentary Politics*. Dublin: Institute of Public Administration.

Seanad Éireann

Seanad Éireann Committee on Procedures and Privileges Sub-Committee on Seanad Reform (2004) *Report on Seanad Reform*. Dublin: Stationery Office.

Civil Service

Dooney, S. and O'Toole, J. (1998) *Irish Government Today* (2nd ed.). Dublin: Gill & Macmillan.

On individual departments

Daly, M. E. (1997) *The Buffer State: The Historical Roots of the Department of the Environment*. Dublin: Institute of Public Administration.

Daly, M. E. (2002) *The First Department: A History of the Department of Agriculture*. Dublin: Institute of Public Administration.

A weighty analysis of the early decades in the development of a central department is provided by Ronan Fanning's *The Irish Department of Finance 1922–58* (Dublin: Institute of Public Administration, 1978).

On public service reform

Collins, N., Cradden, T. and Butler, P. (2007) *Modernising Irish Government: The Politics of Administrative Reform*. Dublin: Gill & Macmillan.

OECD (2008) *Ireland: Towards an Integrated Public Service*. Paris: OECD.

State agencies

Clancy, P. and Murphy, G. (2006) *Outsourcing Government: Public Bodies and Accountability*. Dublin: TASC/New Island.

McGauran, A.-M., Verhoest, K. and Humphreys, P. (2005) *The Corporate Governance of Agencies in Ireland: Non-Commercial National Agencies*. Committee for Public Management Research Report No. 6. Dublin: Institute of Public Administration.

State enterprises
FitzGerald, G. (1963) *State-Sponsored Bodies* (2nd ed.). Dublin: Institute of Public Administration.
National Economic and Social Forum (1980) *Enterprise in the Public Sector.* NESC Report No. 49. Dublin: NESC.

Local government
Callanan, M. and Keogan, J. (eds) (2003) *Local Government in Ireland: Inside Out.* Dublin: Institute of Public Administration.
Roche, D. (1987) *Local Government in Ireland.* Dublin: Institute of Public Administration.

On local and regional agencies
Keyes, J. (2003) 'Community and Enterprise' in M. Callanan and J. Keogan (eds), *Local Government in Ireland: Inside Out.* Dublin: IPA, p. 290.
MacCarthaigh, M. (2007) *The Corporate Governance of Regional and Local Public Service Bodies in Ireland.* CPMR Research Report No. 8. Dublin: Institute of Public Administration.

The Health Services
Curry, J. (2003) *Irish Social Services* (4th ed.). Dublin: Institute of Public Administration, Chapter 5.
Hensey, B. (1988) *The Health Services of Ireland* (4th ed.). Dublin: Institute of Public Administration.
O'Morain, P. (2007) *The Health of the Nation: The Irish Healthcare System 1957–2007.* Dublin: Gill & Macmillan.
Wren, M.-A. (2003) *Unhealthy State: Anatomy of a Sick Society.* Dublin: New Island.

Education
Coolahan, J. (1981) *Irish Education: History and Structure.* Dublin: Institute of Public Administration.
Curry, J. (2003) *Irish Social Services* (4th ed.). Dublin: Institute of Public Administration, Chapter 4.

Justice and the Courts
Doolan, B. (2007) *Principles of Irish Law* (7th ed.). Dublin: Gill & Macmillan.

EU
Callanan, M. (ed.) (2007) *Foundations of an Ever-Closer Union.* Dublin: Institute of Public Administration.

El-Agraa, A. M. (ed.) (2007) *The European Union: Economics and Policies* (8th ed.). Cambridge: Cambridge University Press.

Index